AF687127

Revival

A new kind of Good News and a radically different Promised Land

Six Anti-sermons
from Reverend J. Frank Layman

Revival
A new kind of Good News and a radically different Promised Land
Rev. J. Frank Layman
(written in 2017 and 2018)
(published in 2025)

Cover design by Clayton Pollard
Cover source material: J.D.S / Shutterstock.com

ISBN 979-8-9855830-2-1
UnsafeWords
unsafemedia.com

Contents

Introduction

My name is Reverend J. Frank Layman, and I am a fictional character. A figment of the satirical imagination.

I have been sent here today to spread the gospel of a better world to all who will listen. A world as real as this one, but one that must be chosen. A world that must be won. Not in the name of a God, but in the name of a movement.

In short, I am extending an invitation. An invitation to a new era of technological possibility. An invitation to a renaissance of societal imagination and radical ingenuity. An invitation to a struggle born of vision, commitment, and sacrifice.

Within this heaping helping of Southern fried satire, I'm inviting you to a revolution. And I mean revolution in the truest sense of the word.

We can fundamentally change the way we do things. But, first, we have to fundamentally *rethink* the way we do things.
All of this depends on the questions we are willing to ask.
All of this depends on the questions *you* are willing to ask.

The future I am testifying to does not call for a flock that follows, but rather it depends on a flock who will lead.

My job as a revolutionary shepherd is to nurture a congregation that dismisses dogma, challenges hierarchy, and comprehensively *and resolutely* grasps the urgency in which we must damn the status quo to Hell.

And to those who would interject, "But why a preacher; why *this* type of vessel," I would simply reply, "Why not?"

Certainly we have enough research, reports, and scholarly monographs. Certainly we *have* all the evidence *we need* to break from the path we are on.

And yet here we are. On the edge of a cliff we haven't the courage to peer down deep enough into so we may *see* what the bottom looks like.

Obviously, there are more *traditional* vehicles this information could be conveyed through. But do you really *need* another collection of dry lectures or long-read essays? Do we really need *another* ivory tower tome to place upon the shelf?

Am I saying that I *alone* can make all the difference? Of course not. But I *am* saying that the movement for a better world needs more than mere scholarship. It needs culture and the comfort of common language. It needs charismatic oratory. It needs flair and cadence. It needs storytelling and the aesthetics of prophetic vision.

It needs church.

This is not to say that we need religion, but we *do* need church. In that, we *need* community, we need fellowship, we need pep rallies. We need to come together and strengthen our beliefs. We need to reaffirm our values. And occasionally we need to be reminded what the promised land looks like and what it's going to *take* to get us there.

What I am about to *gift* to you is a small contribution to that church, to this movement, to *our* revolution.

From prayers and prophetic overture to proper damnation of heathens and non-believers, all the way to an offering of salvation and a call to the altar, I will be sharing the gospel of *this* better world in *my own* quite irreverent take on revival style evangelism. A gospel filled with radical truths, grounded hope, and more than the occasional curse word.

Packaged in a series of what I like to call *anti*-sermons, I will draw from a repertoire part poetry, part comedy, and part ZED Talk. Comedy, because comedy is a good bullshit x-ray. Poetry, because what are poems, but prayers to ourselves? And ZED, because this is the *last* fucking thing you're ever going to hear in a TED Talk.

Admittedly, like many preachers, I can at times be overbearing, a little too self-righteous, far too self-assured, and slightly full of shit. Then again, I'm fictional, so I try not to take myself too seriously.

The worth of this contribution, and ultimately the worth of our future, is not going to depend on how well *I* can carry this tune.

It will, however, depend on whether or not *you* are willing to crack open the hymnal and make a joyful noise of your own.

And I don't just mean that figuratively.

In order for you to get the most out of these anti-sermons, you're going to have to participate. You're going to have to put yourself in the right mindset. You're going to have to allow yourself to have fun with it. You're going to have to permit yourself *the freedom* to imagine.

I want you to feel the wood in the pews. I want you to hear the echo in the room. I want you to take *comfort* in the ritual.

I want you to answer the Amens; I want you to feel the Hallelujahs. I want you to contribute to the energy.

I want you to listen *the way one listens* for the few profound words that could change their life.
I want you to respond in *whatever* way the spirit of this moment moves you.

I want you to experience the *magic* of a good old-fashioned revival.
I want to share with you a *new* gospel.
I want you, for the next few hours, to come with me.
To church.

Anti-sermon 01
Prayers and Prophetic Overture

Just a little more space
(Let us pray.)

I want to make
more space for you
to dream
to imagine
to envision.

Just a little more space.

What do you see?
Not the world
but the story.
How did we get there?

What do you see?

Do you see yourself?
Not in that world
but in that story.
How did we get there?

We can get there.

But you have to see yourself.
Not in that world
but in that story.

And we must have
enough space to dream.

(Amen?)

(Amen.)

In search of a collective prophecy
I saw a cartoon one time of this disheveled street prophet holding a sign that read,
"We must avoid the inevitable."

And it got me to thinking about prophecy.
And how prophecy isn't about *avoiding* the inevitable.
It's about preparing us for what comes *after* the inevitable.
It's about what comes after the thing we cannot stop.
All of which is to say that prophecy is ultimately about waiting.

And that is why I believe we need to rethink prophecy.
Because... fuck a bunch of waiting.

Prophecy should not be about the inevitable.
It should be about the possible.

It should not be about predicting the future.
It should be about predicting the futures.
In other words, prophecy shouldn't be about one thing.
It should be about the clarity we possess to see the vastly different array of futures we have before us.

It's about seeing our choice.

With so many asking what kind of future we want, I would ask:
What kind of history do we want?

In other words, how did we get there?

There will be a chapter in our history books about this very moment.
Don't wait to read it.
Write it.

No more waiting for the inevitable.
We need a new kind of prophecy.
One that doesn't predict, one that makes.

We need a collective prophecy.
And we need it now.

(Hallelujah!?!)

(Hallelujah.)

There are different worlds

To understand that there are parallel universes and that each of those universes hinges on our decisions, you don't need a degree in quantum physics. You just need to take out your smartphone and google "bullet trains in Asia" while waiting in line at a Greyhound station in the good old U. S. of A.

There are different worlds.

I'm not here to paint you a photo-realistic picture of what the future is *going* to look like. I'm here to give you a glimpse at a few small fragments shared by a number of different pictures. All of which I believe are far more attractive than, yet every bit as real as, a future of business as usual.

And while these scenarios may be fascinating, it should be said that none of these pictures are new. I am not suggesting anything that hasn't already been alluded to by various philosophers, radical economists, or science fiction writers.

The principles and values in this vision of a better world have been with us for a long long time. What we didn't have before was replicable Open Source Hardware and 3D Printing. What we didn't have before was the Internet of Things for environmental data collection and communication across a network of nodes. What we didn't have before was sophisticated algorithms, data science, and the processing power to handle computations never before imagined. What we didn't have before was Artificial Intelligence and Machine Learning that can master in a matter of hours what it takes humans a lifetime. What we didn't have before was the Blockchain, decentralized and permissionless, to run it all on and introduce an entirely new system.

Before, the only way we could imagine getting to the other side of that door was to risk the consequences of trying to break it down. Now we have the makings of a key.

How we combine these technologies, how we harness their potential, will determine what that key looks like and which door/how many doors we are able to open. In other words, it's more than just the tools.

The tools on their own won't mean shit. It's what we do with them, or what we don't do with them, that matters.

And I would suggest it is what *you* do with what I am saying right here, right now, that matters.
It's how you respond to this call.

You don't have to take my word for it. In fact, I don't want you to take my word for it. I just want you to listen. I want you to listen and feel the weight of what I am saying.

And then I want you to go home and check it out. Do some homework. See for yourself. And when you confirm that all of this, everything I've said, is completely within reach, I want you to ask yourself where you are in all of this.

Think of it like "Where's Waldo," except you're trying to find *yourself* in the picture. On each page of that story, in each different fascinating picture, in each potential future, I want you to locate where you are.

What are *you* doing in that picture?

This is the future of your neighborhood, of your neighborhood, of your neighborhood
There are different worlds.

In one world, we continue to justify whatever consumption the powerful deem fit with terminology like wealth creation, the market, and economic growth.

Yet in a different but very real world, we have amended our concept of consumption.

See, in the future I'm talking about, we've come to acknowledge there's very little *need* to own anything. Instead of mass retail consumption, we've achieved a "temporary-use" society, where almost everything can be checked out and delivered within a matter of minutes, if not seconds, through neighborhood goods libraries that warehouse everything from tools and toys to clothes and sporting equipment to fine china and household cleaners.

Both use and need warrant the production, inventory, and recycling of these goods. Pattern of usage is monitored to ensure availability of items. And whatever items are not already in inventory are ordered from a neighboring goods library facility or supplemented by automated, on-demand 3D printing of open source products.

And for goods and services consumed *outside* the goods library system, things like food and entertainment and travel, you are afforded a combination of various subscription-like reservations.

Said subscriptions offer you full freedom of choice, as well as the ability to input what you would like to see in the research and development of new goods and services.

All surplus goes back into that research and development, as well as insurance/slack budgeting.

All of which is intended to make the process more and more efficient. For the more efficient the process becomes, meaning the more resources saved and waste eliminated, the more everyone is afforded.

There are different worlds.

And in our world, prosperity is no longer measured in terms of growth, but rather through efficiency and sustainability.

Wealth is no longer a matter of amassing objects and symbols of value; wealth is how full we can make our lives in concert with how much of the Earth we are able to save through conservation and innovation.

That world is real, y'all.
That shit can happen.

You can help make that shit happen.
But you have to make that shit happen.

Wham! Just like that

There are different worlds.

In one world, automation and machine learning will displace jobs according to the corporate bottom line, while we will continue to exhaust massive resources in the service of maintaining the system.

Yet in a different but very real world, we say fuck a job, and fuck the system. If fifty million jobs disappear, great. It just means they were obsolete anyway. In our world, jobs are displaced because we no longer see significant portions of the system as necessary.

Instead of marketers, advertisers, and salespeople, we have instituted an easily accessible, non-biased, review clearinghouse for all goods and services.
And wham! Just like that. All of that time is saved. All of those resources are freed.

Instead of banking and a financial industry, we have resource-share algorithms operating on an open, transparent blockchain.
And wham! Just like that. All of that time is saved. All of those resources are freed.

Instead of politicians, lobbyists and public relations firms, we have smart legislation and collective contracts.

And wham! Just like that. All of that time is saved. All of those resources are freed.

Now, in the old way of thinking, such massive loss of industry would be seen as a disaster. But not for us. We see it as a victory.

For, even after automation and machine learning, we will still need human contribution to medicine, science, engineering, architecture, and design. We will still need art, theater, music, literature, poetry, food and drink, laughter, sports, conversation, and sex.

And all the time, talent, and material resources that before had been devoted to making life little more than a secondary concern to that corporate bottom line are now a boon of freed resources, all of which have been shifted toward enhancing the contributions that make life rad as fuck.

Instead of workers left to justify their existence in a system that always deemed them expendable, we allow *all* humans the opportunity to develop their gifts and explore even greater contributions.

And to ensure these opportunities and contributions are not dominated by the privileged, we will implement unlimited, open and free education.

Because whether it's speed reading or dream learning or virtual reality immersion, whether it's plugging information directly into the brain, class hierarchy is going to be difficult to even understand much less be maintained when anyone can learn a trade or skill within a short amount of time. I said when real access to knowledge can no longer be regulated and knowledge itself can no longer be filtered, monopolization of empowering labor can no longer be justified.

And while some most definitely have certain innate gifts that cannot be so easily "downloaded," the point is not to privilege one over the other, but to find a way to efficiently utilize them all.

Instead of a competition for power and individual prizes, our system has instituted social applications and software programs that can facilitate swarm creation and swarm problem solving.

In our world, it's not a matter of who is going to get to do what. It's a matter of everyone contributing and the potential of those contributions being maximized.

There are different worlds.

And that world is real, y'all.
That shit can happen.

You can help make that shit happen.
But you have to make that shit happen.

The real laboratory

Now, again, none of this is brand new. Nor am I claiming this is the inevitable result or even the best result of these technologies.

The internal combustion engine doesn't guarantee a car. Nor does a car *have to* run on an internal combustion engine.

Maybe my idea of a multi-layered subscription model is too shortsighted, especially in light of the eventual goal of post-scarcity. Maybe the goods library is a mere step on the way to everyone having a refrigerator-size 3D printer and recycler in their home.

Maybe we need less vision from folks like me and more experimentation from folks like you. Maybe the real magic is going to be abracadabraed in the streets.

As much as the privileged, like myself, demonstrate the propensity to pontificate on what revolution could look like, a lot of the real legwork is going to be done by those with the least resources and/or those on the margins.

Because it's not just the invention that matters. It's the modification of that invention. And a good deal of that modification, that pragmatic adaptation, is going to result from a hustle. Regular folks on the grind, learning and using these new tools to get by. Not in theory but in necessary practice.

From fashion to art to all aspects of the underground economy, the *real* laboratory for social innovation is in the streets. There's no reason to believe *this* innovation is any different.

The first few syllables of tech-speak

The problem is that so few people know this shit is even an option. And while I get that the average Joe and Jolene aren't up to speed on the latest developments in artificial intelligence, how many so-called revolutionaries know almost nothing (or, even worse, just don't give a fuck) about how technology fits into our potential of winning a better world? How many roll their eyes at the ignorant and/or apathetic masses but then allow those same eyes to glaze over after the first few syllables of tech-speak?

Sure, these technologies are in their infancy. But if you've been walking for three days in the desert and it just started to sprinkle, that's some exciting shit.

And yet so many of us aren't paying attention to the manna clouds right above our heads.
No wonder why this shit is hard for the average Joe or Jolene to imagine.

And if you *are* having trouble imagining any of what I have described being harmoniously introduced into our culture, *any* of this vision actually becoming the norm, keep in mind there is an entire generation already born that will never know life without a smartphone. And the same for every generation after.

That is a big goddamn leap. And to continue to deny the role that technology *is* going to play in this movement? Well, that's just you demonstrating your mere preference for the old way of doing things. I said any self-described revolutionary who ignores the power offered by this array of new technologies is like the asshole who prefers dittos and faxes over holograms.

There are different worlds.

And it is not just the average Joe or Jolene that needs convincing of that. Sometimes it is the radicals themselves.

If we are to be anything more than smugly self-righteous, if we are to be taken any more seriously than the establishment know-it-alls who constantly tell us that there is no alternative, we have to be aware of all that the physical world has to offer us.

We cannot claim to want a better world and not wholeheartedly embrace the tools we have to build it.

That world *is* real.
It can really happen.
It can finally happen.

You can help make that shit happen.
But you have to make that shit happen.

The quality of our brushes
(Let us pray.)

If the pictures that we are painting
seem abstract
if the places that we are describing
seem out of reach

think about
today's most advanced technologies
as well as the advancements that will soon
be obsolete.

Imagine
someone at the inception
of those developments
painting a picture
of right now.

Would that picture not have also
appeared
out of reach?

As we improve
the quality of our brushes

these paintings will look
less and less

abstract.

(Amen?)

(Amen.)

Hellfire and Brimstone

This kind of change doesn't require that we be experts. It requires that we be urgent. And yet - artificial intelligence, robotic automation, and the internet of things are still in their infancy. If you're having trouble imagining how *good* things can get, it's understandable. It's understandable if none of this seems all that urgent.

But if I make one *real* prediction in all of this, it is that status quo development of these technologies will not result in a better world; it will result in a worse one. And if you're having trouble imagining how *bad* that worse world can get, well, there's just no excuse for it.

Ignorance is ours to overcome.
What we should not have to overcome is willful ignorance.

Now, the only thing I know that can arouse urgency in the face of obstinance is fear. And as a former believer, as a former fundamentalist believer, fear is one thing I keenly understand.

I said, as a former believer, I know how many Christians have chosen Heaven out of fear over the alternative.

So I ask: Why not opt for a little Just-In-Case Salvation here on Earth?

I mean do I really need to convince you where the status quo is headed? I am acutely aware that no self-respecting Southern preacher would be caught dead without a little Hellfire and Brimstone in their sermon. But do I really need to paint that picture for you?

Do I need to go into the gory details of what blockchain and crypto super scams will look like, of what a closed internet and social credit scoring will look like, of what post-automation serfdom will look like, of what neuro-policing will look like?
Do I really have to warn you of the flames up ahead?

Or do I just have to ask you to be honest?
Be honest about the world we live in right now, the system we live in right now.

Tell the truth and shame the Devil. Do you want this technology in the hands of the same people, the same system, that prefer weapons sales to security and sue poor countries over the right of rich countries to patent away life-saving medicines? The same leaders who boast about sanctioning half a million children to death and start wars over fucking bananas? The same assholes who have already allowed climate change to ensure mass extinction of plant and animal species and have taken humanity to the brink of the point of no return?

Do you really think the powerful are going to play nice with all these new toys?

It's not the unknown that you have to fear. It is what you know.

It is what you already know about the Hell ahead of us that should hasten your acceptance of salvation.

You can continue to feign ignorance. You can continue to do nothing. You can continue to put your faith in the status quo and watch what is left of our decency fall apart.

Or you can believe in something more. You can put your faith in something better. You can be saved.

I am offering salvation, in that I am offering you the *chance* to save yourself by contributing to a better world. I am offering you the chance to save those who come after you by contributing to a better world. I am offering you this chance to be honest about what you know.

As one who has squirmed in the pews more times than I care to remember, I know that most Hellfire and Brimstone sermons are taught from the Book of Revelation.

And upon reading the Book of Revelation, you are meant to ask yourself, "Where am I going to be when Judgment Day comes? Will my name appear in the Book of Life?"

Well, I say Judgment Day is today.
And it is not about the judgment of a God or the followers of a religion.
It is about your own judgment, the one you make *right now.*

The question is not: "Where am I going to be on so and so day?"
The question is: "Where am I right now?"

Do not wait for someone else's prophecy to be fulfilled. Identify the future you want and the story of how we got there, and write your name in *that* book right now. Right. God. Damn. Now.

A People's History of the Future

Now, I hate to break this to you so late in the sermon. But if you came here for answers, you came to the wrong place. I'm not even smart enough to give you the right questions. But I do understand enough to know that I have an obligation to do everything I can to get *you too* to start asking.

I'm not here to give you the technical specs for revolution. I'm not here to give you the step-by-step instructions for revolution. I'm here to give you the desire to go find out that shit. I'm here to give you the incentive to go after that shit. I'm here to give you the obligation to make that shit happen.

I can't tell you what your future is going to look like. Because there's infinite ways it *could* turn out. What I *can* do is give you a real possibility, or a few real possibilities, that are desirable as fuck and unleash your hungry asses on that tasty future.

I'm not here to lead the way. I'm here to light a fire. I'm here to offer this movement a little culture. I'm here to make a little more space for you to dream.

Because, see, this isn't about me. And, frankly, it's not about you either, at least not who you are right now. It's about who you're going to become. And by who you're going to become, I mean how you are going to contribute to who *we* are going to become.

We can get to a better world. The emergence of this new technology now allows the puzzle pieces to more easily fit together. I want each of *you* to craft your own piece of that puzzle and find where that piece fits in.

But I'm not here to tell you how to do it. You're here to tell me how to do it.
I'm just here to tell you to tell me how to do it.

I'm here to make a call.

As Howard Zinn proved, the people who write history often determine the people who "make" history.

Let's not wait to read someone else's account of how we got *here.* Let's tell our brothers and sisters in that beautiful *better* future how *we* got them *there.*

If there had been no Howard Zinn, that history would still have existed.
That's why he called it a *People's* History. Because it was theirs.

They wrote it. Every step of the way.

He was just there to help us bear witness.

Making history isn't about taking credit. It's about understanding history's worth and your place in it.

The only history worth being told is one that gives you the clearest picture possible of how much you owe. Not just to those before you, but those after you. The only history worth being heard is one that lets you know it is possible to pay that debt.

We owe so much, y'all. To those before us, and to those after us.

Let's find our place in the story.
Let's pay that debt.

Let's write a People's History of the Future.

And let's do it right now.

Anti-sermon 02
Proper Damnation of Heathens and Non-believers

Don't let them tell you
(Let us pray.)

Don't let them tell you
it can't happen.

It's another way of telling you
you ain't shit
that you ain't nothing
that you better stay in your place
that you better ask
no, you better beg
for what they give you

and be happy
it was so much.

You don't need them
to tell you
a goddamn thing.

That shit can happen
just like it happened us ending up here.

The only thing you need
is to figure out
what it is

you're telling yourself.

(Amen?)

(Amen.)

There's always some cynical asshole

One of the problems with revolution, including this revolution (and I would go as far as to say especially this revolution), is that whenever you start talking about revolution, there's always some cynical asshole who's generous enough with his or her (usually his) wisdom to enlighten you as to why that shit ain't never gonna happen.

And my first reaction to these particular generous assholes is that they are no better than the politicians who lament the inevitability of mass shootings or the economists who have for decades called Universal Healthcare a fantasy, when in both cases the starkest of realities in almost every other industrialized nation on the planet is, and has been for a long time, the complete opposite.

There were different ways we could have gone with train technology and its infrastructure, with automobile technology and its infrastructure, with bicycle technology and its infrastructure. There are different ways we *could* go with drone technology and its infrastructure.

Nevertheless, we, or should I say each geographic we, always only end up in one place. In one precise direction.

And, if nothing else, I simply wish to point out the different number of paths there are to take and how much more desirable some of those paths are, and yes how possible they are. Maybe not as probable, but possible nonetheless.

Having said that, there will most certainly be an array of know-it-alls and adults in the room to take a self-righteous dump on the vision this movement is attempting to give life. And it is crucial to that vision that this movement addresses how to deal with such naysayers.

Dumbing down the future: The Improbability Squad

The first of which I refer to as the Improbability Squad. Those who basically want to dumb down the future as a way of hedging their bets. Those who can explain in vivid detail the revolutionary promise of this technology, only to adorn such findings with an *utterly anguished* endorsement of why it probably *won't* happen.

By flirting with the possibility, and yes even the desirability, of this vision, they can take *all* the credit if any such flirtations bear fruit. While, at the same time, preemptively saving face if it all falls to shit.

They're like a door-to-door salesperson who starts out their pitch with "hey, look at all this hope" but then closes with "but what really *is* hope anyway?"

Fancying themselves to be realists, what they *really* are is comfortable. For this kind of hedging can only be made from a position of privilege. Those who believe the status quo is not risky enough to go all in against it.

Because the truth is: those who do not *commit* to winning are content with losing.

Now, while some of such self-described realists will blame our *probable* shortcomings on the unforeseen limits of the technology, others simply foresee us being outmaneuvered by the powerful. One too lazy to imagine, the other too pragmatic/cowardly to fight.

But my favorite of the bunch are the ones who just come out and say what the other two groups are already thinking. That we must not really *want it* bad enough.

You know who I'm talking about. Those who tell us that they *absolutely* share our longing for a better world and that these ideas are all well and good, but unfortunately there's just not enough *political will* to make that kind of change a reality.

But here's the thing. If you really gave a shit about political will, you would be a *wee bit more* focused on how this technology offers us a chance to make political will far more efficient and self-determination far easier. A chance we would *never* have without such technology.

Or does the only political will *you're concerned with* just happen to be the one which has been thoroughly neutered by the designated spokesmodels within the political class?

Because, folks, it doesn't take a terminal degree and tenure to see that discounting a technology's potential due to the present vision of a propagandized populace is not merely backwards; it's self-defeating.

And yet somehow they have the audacity to deem it courageous when they dismiss the probability of real change due to the *current* lack of political will.
But it is not courageous. It is conniving.
You *know* how change works.
And you *know* it is not probable *until* you can demonstrate that political will.
It is not probable unless you can *create* that political will.

Obviously, the political will doesn't *currently* exist.
But does that mean our only option is to take this technology, which again is in its infancy, and relegate it to whatever use the status quo can find for it?

Do we sit back and hope *a really heavy hope* that the powers that be *will be* benevolent enough to not use these new miracles of science to take away what little self-determination we have left?

Or do we set out to *create* the kind of political will that frankly doesn't give a fuck what the powers that be think?

Well, I don't know about you, but I'm tired of sitting around waiting to win the benevolence lottery. I say that instead of surrendering our future livelihoods to the current absence of political will, we treat political will like it is a fucking jobs program in itself, and actively recruit people for all the positions that are currently unfilled.

(Amen?)

(Amen.)

Scaredy Cats: But what if you're wrong

Now, if the "Improbability Squad" wasn't disappointing enough, then you've got the "be careful what you wish for" assholes.

The sarcastic Scaredy Cats who far too easily emulate the emptiest of our religious zealots, those who do not even bother hiding their snickers as they implore of their atheist brethren, "But what if you're wrong? Hmm hmm hmm. You might wind up in Hell."

As if we're not already in Hell. Granted, not everyone is on the same level of Hell. But look the fuck around. When we're losing animal species and coral reef faster than conspiracy theorists lose their chance of getting laid and the doomsday clock is only a cock hair away from puking up a cuckoo bird, we're not exactly camped outside the pearly gates.

Obviously, things *could* get worse. No one is denying another level of Hell exists. We just believe that if we do nothing, we're going to end up in that next level anyway.

And yet when we come to you and say, "Hey, man. I think I've got a plan to get us out of Hell," all your silly asses can say is, "Yeah, but what if it's really hot *out there*?"

Scaredy Cats: Wallowing in the danger

Of course, those are mostly people who don't even care to understand the technology. Rather than make the effort to learn a few new vocabulary words, it's easier to just treat the science as a potential bogeyman and feign fear of the unknown.

The real group of Scaredy Cats, though, are those who believe they already know the unknown and fear the technology because they think they understand it all too well.

Like cave dwellers who saw right through the beguiling promise of fire the first time their hand got too close to the flame, they scold us for our excitement and dismiss our plans as delusions of desperate grandeur.

And while it is true that the discovery of fire did not directly lead to flying cars and jetpacks, those who *rightly* warn against the fetishization of these technologies must themselves resist the temptation to wallow in their dangers.

It goes without saying, the technologies are not our savior. They are just another set of tools. But they are a set of tools we've never had before.

And you don't protect people by making them afraid of their tools. You help them envision what can be built, what *they* can build.

If you want to focus on the horrors that *could* spring out of these new technologies, then let *that focus* be a driver for a *different* vision; let it be an urgent call to *counter* the status quo.

Your fear of the technology is really just a fear of a world where it's business as usual. The technology is on the way, whether we like it or not. And to illuminate the probability of losing *without* the possibility of winning is worse than any fetishization. It is defeatism.

Pointing out the speeding truck barreling toward the baby carriage doesn't make you a fucking hero. In fact, what most of this talk amounts to is pointing out the speeding truck as a mere means to the end of arguing that there's really no use in trying to move the baby carriage out of the way.

It also ignores who's driving the truck. Because those assholes aren't asleep at the wheel. They've got their foot on the gas.

The cold reality is if we don't win, those assholes are going to win. So stop telling us we can't win.

The only reason why this shit is considered a pipe dream is because motherfuckers like you convince people of it. You soften the blow of defeat and limit the expectation of those fighting, and you do it as if you're performing some kind of service. When the only service you're performing is for those who would sooner crush us and everyone we love than they would crush a can for recycling.

Unless we are prepared to integrate these new technologies into our struggle, unless we are thirsty for their revolutionary potential, we're going to enter the future bringing a rock to a laser fight.

To merely be *aware* of the dangers of these new technologies is defensive at best. But defensive in the next era is futile as fuck. It's not even reformist; it's survivalist.

We might as well just say fuck it and go jump off a bridge.

The prescription is not to hide our luddite heads in the corporate quicksand.
The prescription is a sober understanding of how the technology works *and* how power works.

This is not an either/or situation.

We can walk and chew bubble gum at the same time as we're pulling off a revolution.

(Amen?)

(Amen.)

That could never happen
And still, as irritating as the Improbability Squad is, as frustrating as the Scaredy Cats are, none of them hold a candle to the *real* adults in the room. Those who profess to believe that this could simply *never* happen.

Those who have gotten to a place where being smart enough to dazzle our dumbasses with ten minutes of hope at a TED Talk was no longer enough to get them off. I said those who now know the real prize is the pride of having seen this hope coming a mile away and having so easily shot it down.

And yet these geniuses, so quick to rain shit on our parade, are the most lazy and unimaginative of the bunch.

They point to early failures or missteps as evidence of improbability or perhaps even a fatal flaw, essentially blaming the tools for what some asshole did with the tools. They laugh at the shortsightedness of someone not seeing all the obstacles, while ignoring the culture of trial and error in all technological progress.

And while you are describing our optimism as naive, our vision as naive, I would just remind you that these developments are at such an early stage it is almost impossible to foresee what kinds of breakthroughs will be accumulated at the edges. Thus it is *quite* naive to infuse such wildly pessimistic claims with any rational confidence.

Yet it is their *confidence* they depend on, not their rationality. For they can only sound *this* smart as long as they can convince us there is no use in even *attempting* to prove them wrong.

In other words, they are just one more group whose view of the world *depends* on how many heads they can stand upon to see it.

Well, I say no more. No more elevating those who tell us that our only hope is to curry favor with the right barbarian, that our true mission is to fight for the last spot in a choir that sings praises to a murderous system in exchange for its occasional sparing of charity.

I say no more. No more.

The message is the same

Now, I could go on giving you examples of how they will tell us this vision could never happen. But the purpose of this sermon is not to lay out the definitive list of naysayers. The purpose of this sermon is to highlight a trend that runs through them all.

For almost all of them give at least some lip service to the absolute foolishness of doing nothing. Yet their solutions sound less like rallying cries and more like a lament. *"For, my friends, what choice do we have but to piss into the wind?"*

On the one hand, they acknowledge that ignoring the potential of this technology is a dangerous political act. But then they turn around and tell people not to expect too much from this technology, which again is in its infancy, as if that is not an enormous political act.

It's like this tightrope walk of trying to appear moral while still painting the neo-liberal trajectory of this technology as all but a given, implying our only realistic goal is to find a more comfy seat on the doom train.

Between the assholes who think Franz Kafka was too cheery and the assholes whose version of optimism is "brace for impact," the message is pretty much the same: Know your limitations, and don't even think about winning.

It's this go-slightly-against-the-flow reformism that pleads with us not to dream too big. As if being disappointed that we didn't *win it all* would somehow be worse than just accepting the future allowance of dignity we will be allotted within the proverbial prison walls.

And I don't even know why we bother pretending they're on our side. I mean we certainly aren't going to *win it all* with that mediocre-ass pep talk.

Of course, they're *not* concerned with winning. They're simply meeting the minimum for what it takes to *feel* like they are not part of the problem and still save face in case they're wrong. They're doing *just enough* to keep their progressive credentials, but *also enough* to keep their career goals.

It reminds me of the consultants who advise politicians to start their negotiations in the middle and then act surprised when they get almost none of what they wanted. Only then to charge even higher rates for their expertise the next election cycle.

And you wonder why there are radical assholes like me out here talking revolution.

Because, see, I'll admit I want to overshoot expectations by ridiculous leaps of the imagination, so anything even remotely close looks like a goddamn Utopia.

That's right. Fuck starting in the middle. And fuck negotiation too. This is a better world we're talking about. We don't have to negotiate shit.

We just have to make it happen.

(Hallelujah!?!)

(Hallelujah.)

And who knows? Maybe you really believe that we can't make it happen. Maybe for you *every* day is the end of the line for technology, every breakthrough is obviously the last breakthrough. Maybe you really do believe that.

Or maybe this is just a way for you to make everything about me me me. The Grand Know-It-All writing another New York Times best-seller of arrogant self-fulfilling prophecies. All that education, all that intellectual energy, all that time, all of it spent on a chance at winning the Golden I Told You So. Maybe that's what this is *for you.*

Either way, you've got to know: Since the dawn of applied science, there have been people *just like you* making relatively the same points you're making right now at the infancy of each breakthrough technology.

You know there were. You just don't know their names.

In other words, no one ever made the history books for being the know-it-all asshole who pointed out why some shit couldn't happen. That's right. No one ever got famous for predicting why the future *wasn't* possible.

If we want a better world, and for some that seems to be a big *if*, but if we truly want a better world, the goal is not to point out how difficult something would be; it's to figure out how it could be made less difficult.

And while I agree that identifying the problem is crucial, a lot of y'all treat that shit like it's the finish line.

We don't need to dull the expectations of tomorrow's Nikola Tesla by smugly highlighting the limitations of technologies that, I repeat, are still in their fucking infancy. We need them to believe they can solve all these problems. I said we need to start a fucking fire under a generation of Nikola Teslas. We need to start a fire under a generation of educated dreamers. And, with our principles, with our values, we need to point that generation in the direction of a better world.

(Amen?)

(Amen.)

A toast to the unsung heroes of our revolution

And yet, I have come to see now that my first reaction to write off these naysayers was wrong. I initially viewed them as being no better than the racist uncle back in the 80s who used to go on and on about how rap music would never last.

But then I realized my reaction was also shortsighted, and that if all I did was heap scorn and ridicule upon what I see in them as a waste of talent, I would be guilty of the same crime. I would be guilty of not seeing the *real* value in what is right in front of me.

We have to see the value in *everything* available to us.

There are always going to be people who throw rocks at the plausibility, or even the possibility, of radical vision. And those people, even in their innate inclination for the overbearing, are valuable. They are valuable in that they devote all their brilliance and analytical wit to finding the myriad of circumstances that would prevent such a future from realization. In other words, they are the ones who point out our tasks, our challenges to overcome.

When someone says that could never happen because of this big, bad problem, what they're really saying is - that could never happen because we haven't solved the problem *yet*.

Think of it as a matter of translation.

When someone tells us "XYZ can't be done," we need to hear "we haven't figured out how to do XYZ *yet*." And then we have to figure out how to do XYZ.

Just remember, don't let them tell you our shit is doomed without also telling you why. If we're going to pay the price of listening to these clever motherfuckers wax poetic about our demise, they *have* to tell us the wrong turns we took to get there.

Lucky for us, by nature such assholes take delight in being obnoxious. And the only thing more obnoxious than halting someone's epic journey is laying out a riddle that must be solved in order to pass.

Having said all that, as long as we are willing to pay the price of admission and they are willing to give us that ticket, I see no need to hold ill will against these curmudgeons of vision.

In fact, I believe it is better to embrace them. I would even go as far as to celebrate them.

Let them be as cynical as they want. As long as they are accurate in pointing out our pitfalls, they will have performed a real service in the revolution. And a thankless one at that.

For even if they don't know they're doing it, *we* must acknowledge the selflessness of their actions.

To ghost write such a grand and mystifying tale is a dirty job. But somebody has to do it. And these intellectuals, these experts, these futurists, in their monumental condescension, are willing to make that sacrifice.

And that, my friends, is why I believe a toast is in order. A tribute, if you will, to the towering figures of the unwitting vanguard.

Those who threw the alley-oop while proclaiming the rim was too high for anyone to ever dunk.

Those who knew just enough to set the table, all so someone else could serve the meal.

Let us raise our glasses to these overbearing know-it-alls.
The insight so priceless. The irony so lost.

When we get there, we'll say, "We couldn't have done it without them."

And everyone's response will be, "Who the fuck are you talking about?"

Here's to you, you beautiful pricks.
You are, and will always be, the unsung heroes of our revolution.

Salute!

So who the fuck are you?
"So who the fuck are you?"
"Why are you even doing this?"
"Why should anyone listen to you?"
That's what some of you are thinking, isn't it?
Why do *I* think I know more than the experts?

And it's a legitimate question. Because I'm not an expert. I don't even have any degrees. I'm little more than a library anarchist trying to pull off bad performance art while holding down a shitty, low-paying day job.

But if you really want to know. The reason why you should pay attention to my silly ass is the same reason I came up with the idea for these anti-sermons.

See, I remember when I heard about the blockchain for the first time. A buddy of mine told me I needed to check this shit out and that it was going to be big. So I did what a lot of us do, and I went online and found a bunch of lectures and presentations, including a few TED Talks.

And after watching a few of these, I started to feel like a high school English teacher tasked with reading twenty-five of the same book report. It was like every guru or expert on the subject had really just watched two other TED Talks and translated it into their own address format. There was no *real* insight. Just this rehash of bullet points, with a few witty comments thrown in for style points.

What they were saying was informative, but it wasn't important. Now, that's not to say the information wasn't important, but *how* they were delivering that information was just not important.

When you're talking about a breakthrough that could end up evolving into something more consequential than the internet, you need more than book report style recycling of knowledge.

You need someone who's going to stand up in front of an audience of complete strangers and "O Captain, my Captain" those motherfuckers, leaving everybody in the room running out of the room so they can hurry up and get home and start writing their own chapter on the subject.

The point of doing this is to provide the space for *all* of us to imagine the bridge between here and there. It is to get you fired up, anxious to identify the spots in that bridge that need filling, the openings, large or small, that you might just be able to fill.

That's what I'm trying to do with these anti-sermons. That's what I'm trying to do with all of this.

And look, I get it. I'm a nobody. And these people are all way smarter than I'll ever be.
So if you don't want to listen to my take on this shit, you obviously don't have to.

But just go watch some of these lectures, some of these interviews. Go read their books. I mean that literally. I tell people that. Go read their books. Because these are smart people, and some of them have done really great work in laying out the nuts and bolts of these technologies. And that is something I would never be able to do.

But when you take in all this amazing information, and then you look at what the major debates are about, it's completely underwhelming.

Because it's not that there *aren't* experts out there that get it, that know this shit can happen. There are. They exist. They're out there. But what do they do when the microphone is put in their hand? They half-ass it. Even when they do say something that is inspiring or visionary, they shoot too low.

Take a look at what the experts are excited about right now.

Take automation, for example. We've known for quite some time now that automation is soon going to be sophisticated enough to put so many people out of work that if we don't do something to counter that shit, there won't be bread lines. There'll be bread riots.

And yet the farthest that most of these fucking geniuses can see down the road is the Universal Basic Income, or some dressed up version of the Universal Basic Income.

When, if we're really fucking honest, the Universal Basic Income is primarily intended to save capitalism. It's New Deal 2.0 shit.

That shit ain't radical; that shit is tepid. That shit ain't visionary; that shit is inevitable. And what I mean by that is, if neoliberals want to avoid having to make the darkest of decisions, the Universal Basic Income is going to happen in one form or another.

Now, would the UBI provide some real relief for people who are struggling? Absolutely it would. Like most reforms, it would address real human suffering and immediate human needs. And that is a good thing.

But that shit should be seen as merely one step in our dance. The Universal Basic Income should be viewed as only one punch in a combination of punches, a combination of punches that must be thrown or else we're going to lose the fucking fight.

Because unless you address the system that led us to this point, a Universal Basic Income isn't going to provide us with any more real bargaining power than we had before. And in fact it may leave us with less. So when automation does kick in and the powers that be decide to start whittling away at what's left of our education, healthcare, infrastructure, civil rights, and yes even the dollar amount of the UBI itself, where the fuck are we going to go?

You have to address the system. You have to address the structure of our economy. You have to address the structure of our politics. You have to address the technologies themselves.

We're going to have to figure out how to use our collective resources to invest in automation that no longer works for their greedy asses, but literally works for us. And even that is just a step in the dance.

If we're going to have a Universal Basic Income, and it looks like we probably will, we have to think of it as one step. We can't think of a UBI as the future. We have to think of it as a temporary layover to what comes after.

I mean just look at the language we're using to describe what so many see as the future. The word "Income" implies the same system. It implies that we need an income, so we can then go out and spend that income in the market. But that shit ain't the future; that's the past.

Instead of thinking in terms of a Universal Basic Income, why not think in terms of a Universal Basic Share, where we *all* have an equitable and sustainable distribution of the resources our planet has to offer.

And you know what? While you're at it, take the word "Basic" out. We don't want something that is merely basic. We want something that is just. And if we want a system that is just, then I say we call it a Universal Just Share. Or we could even shorten it to a "Just Share." Get it? *Just Share!*

You have to address the system, and you have to address the system in the context of these new technologies. We're not asking you to predict what technologies will come along in half a century. We're just trying to take a fucking inventory of what we have right now.

Because again, most of what we need to make that shit happen already exists. Even if it's in its infancy, it fucking exists.

And yet the best that most of these experts can do is see about 1 ½ steps into the future. When the real excitement is 4 or 5 steps into the future. And what is equally exciting is how we get to that future, how we overcome these challenges. That shit is exciting.

Yet that shit is not what the experts are going to talk about in their fucking TED Talk. That shit is not what the futurists are going to talk about in their TED Talk.

And by the way, the futurists are the fucking worst. Futurists are the fucking worst!
And why?
Because while at the same time futurists can describe a world ahead that is almost unrecognizable to what we knew two decades ago, they will make sure to insist it will be under the same economic model we had two centuries ago.

Which makes total sense when you consider who funds most of our futurists.

Because when the people who sign their paychecks hear about these new technologies, they don't want their vision to be clouded by words like "decline in wages" or "loss of jobs." They want their vision to be made up of words like "growth" and "wealth creation."

That's why, just like so many of our other experts, these so-called futurists churn out all this high school book report bullshit. Because their vision is limited to the same frame as our economists.

It's like futurists have become the economists of prophecy.

When the only real future these motherfuckers are concerned with is their next speaking engagement or their next book contract. They know if they start looking into any unapproved crystal balls, *their* future will be easy to predict.

Well, guess what? I don't have any speaking fees to risk. I don't have any mainstream publishers to lose.

And that's why I can do what I do.
And that's why I'm doing what I'm doing.

The problem is, beyond my evangelizing, it doesn't matter what the fuck I do, because I have zero skills for any of this shit.

Fortunately, there's a good number of folks, a whole lot smarter than me, that *are* already on the path. But without a whole lot more folks getting involved, it ain't gonna matter what they're doing either.

It matters what you do right now. Whatever kind of contribution you have to offer, it matters. Even if you don't know what that contribution is going to look like, you have to know that it *will* matter.

Don't leave the future to the futurists. Don't leave it to the TED Talkers. Don't leave it to the Improbability Squad or the Scaredy Cats.

It's your goddamn future as much as it is theirs. But only if you own it, only if you go after something more.

Don't let them tell you this shit can't happen.
Don't let them tell you a goddamn thing.
Don't let them dumb down our future.

Anti-sermon 03
An Offering of Salvation (Part One): But Can I Get Rich

Why do you feel that
(Let us pray.)

You are not capitalism.
You are not capitalism.
You are not capitalism.
You are not capitalism.

So why do you feel that
impulse?
The need to defend, to counter.
That reflex to dismiss, to deride.
Why do you feel that?

You are not capitalism.

You are not capitalism any more than you are monarchy
or theocracy
or fascism.
You could have been born into any of these.
You were born into
capitalism.

But you
are not capitalism.

So when you hear these words
ask yourself,
"Why do I feel that?"

(Amen?)

(Amen.)

Getting beyond the Cold War
If you assume from the previous two sermons or the prayer I just read that I am an anti-capitalist, you're missing the point. I don't consider myself an anti-capitalist. I simply want to get *beyond* capitalism. I want to get *beyond* capitalism just like I would want to get beyond Soviet-style planning, had it endured.

I have no interest in economic debates from the Cold War. That shit is the past. Arguing over which is the best economy for yesterday is like jacking off, a fun but otherwise unproductive exercise.

We need to put to bed all the assumptions that lie within that old debate and start from the inevitable predicament in which automation and all manner of artificial intelligence are going to place us.

It is from within the frame of these evolving circumstances, as well as that of our newfound possibilities, which we must start this new debate.

But to even enter that debate, we are going to have to take a long look at ourselves and affirm what we are and what we are not.

And we are not, *you* are not, capitalism.

An arranged marriage
Why do we feel so wrong asking these questions? Why does it feel like we're being unfaithful to a partner?

Because you need to know that your fidelity to capitalism is a gamble. And you need to think about what that gamble is really based on.

In the face of challenges we couldn't imagine two decades before, you won't recognize that soulmate of yours two decades from now.

Furthermore, you didn't fall in love with capitalism. What you remember as romance was always an arranged marriage.

The truth is: we don't have a human or spiritual connection to capitalism. We have a sentimental connection to the brand that capitalism has become.

I want to get past the brands and the symbols that anchor us to antiquation and try to imagine what human dignity looks like within the context of these new tools and this new century.

I am not anti-capitalist. I want to go beyond capitalism.

What more do you need

Now, they ask, "Why is it so important for you to go beyond capitalism?"
And I ask, "Why is it so important for you to stay?"

The number one reason *we* didn't stop climate change in its tracks is because capitalism offered just enough incentive not to stop it.
Not even the truest free market believers can refute that statement.

So what else is there to say?
What more do you need?

You're free to spend your time trying to find enough good to balance out a system that put us on the brink of destruction.

But if the vision we're describing is possible, why would you *want* to keep capitalism around?

Why is it so important for you to stay?

You don't have to stay

You don't have to stay with capitalism.
You don't owe capitalism your love.

You don't have to worry about capitalism's feelings.
You don't have to let capitalism down easy.
You don't have to worry about what's going to happen to capitalism.

You can just walk away.

If you want to keep a picture, that's fine.
Just make sure it is a clear one.

(Amen?)

(Amen.)

Like all myth turned faith
I used to think it was sentimental.
Now I think it is superstition.

How else could so many people support such a horrendous story of human division?

Since the Corporation became the new Adam, we have convinced ourselves that this economic model is a *super*natural order. A religion, where Wall Street is the church and the so-called "free market" is its deity. The wealthy are the saints, the economists are the prophets, the executives are the priests, the politicians are the ushers, the media are the choir, and the flock is the middle class and working poor who worship at the altar.

The flock are told to focus. Not on their current hardships, but rather on the mansions and streets of gold promised down the line.

For in this faith, morality is money, and hope is only allowed in prayer requests.
In this faith, the golden rule is competition, and the pursuit of capital is the sole measure of devotion.
In this faith, the rich are the righteous and the poor are the sinners. Winners and losers. The chosen and the heathen.
In this faith, fundamentalism is rewarded, and parables are to be taken literally.
In this faith, the Word is handed down, and doubting the Word is a dangerous, dangerous sin.

Like all deities before it, the free market is to be worshipped. And like all myth turned faith, no one's ever seen it, but everyone knows what it looks like.
And everyone knows how good it is.
And everyone knows that it is coming to save us.

For sinners can only be saved by giving themselves to the free market and graciously accepting their suffering. Sinners can only be saved by kneeling down before the saints.

Should I go on? Or does that just about sum it up?

Is that not the dogma we are asked to commit to, to rehearse, to repeat over and over, all for the sake of ritual? Is that not why we have such a hard time imagining a world without capitalism, a life without capitalism? Is that not why we feel something is wrong whenever we find ourselves silently siding with the heretics, those who merely suggest that something is wrong?

What could this be, if not faith? For only faith can make you feel guilt at the thought of entertaining a question.

And our understanding of that guilt, our comprehension of this special kind of irrationality, our grasp of this faith, is going to be absolutely crucial in the times to come. For it is not just devotion to the free market that we have to worry about.

Although this technology is in its infancy, there are already people rushing to literally worship at the altar of this new science, ready to submit to the new deity of Artificial Intelligence.

And surely such a phenomenon would seem surreal had we not already treated capitalism like a religion for over a century.

The folly that led us to seek salvation in the life given to an economic philosophy is the same folly that will find us surrendering to the life given to technology.

It is salvation through surrender. And it is folly.

We must recognize that folly before it is too late.
We must *all* recognize that folly before it's too late.

(Let us pray.)

You
are not capitalism.

(Amen?)

(Amen.)

It is not the technology that is coming for us
Of course, while some are running to worship, there are an increasing number of prominent thinkers urging us to run away. Fearing what the science may bring. Scared the technology is coming for us.

But it is not the technology that is coming for us. It is capitalism that is coming for us. We only need fear the technology to the extent we fear the context in which it will be designed and implemented. For us, that context is capitalism.

Additionally, there are those who predict this technology will eventually make humans irrelevant. But doesn't an economic system where, by law, profits must be put before people *already* make humans irrelevant?

It is not *that* life will be breathed into the machines; it is what that life will look like. Will it look like the life we already breathed into capitalism, making its institutions self-sustaining? Isn't that actually the life we dread, now fearful of its technological offspring?

Again, concerns about the science are ultimately concerns about capitalism.

And our task is neither to police nor persuade the engineers.

Our task is to take a life. Or rather to take back the life we breathed into capitalism. It is to dismantle those institutions. It is to rethink

and replace each tenet we've come to believe is a natural order. And it is to do so as quickly as possible.
Before it really is too late.

(Let us pray.)

You
are not capitalism.

(Amen?)

(Amen.)

The press conference
I want you to imagine a global press conference held by scientists in the 1970s, the purpose of which was to explain the science behind human-induced climate change, to present the evidence of human-induced climate change.

And then I want you to imagine this 1970s press conference concluding with the lead scientist telling the world that there's no sense in trying to stop human-induced climate change, or even to lessen the pace of human-induced climate change. That we instead need to focus our efforts on the year 2020 and how we might adapt to the onslaught of catastrophic weather events.

And as the gasps fill the room, a reporter stands up and asks, "Are you saying we have no way of preventing this from happening?"

And the scientist says, "Well, of course we have the ability to prevent it. We just won't."

And the reporter says, "But that's fifty years in the future."

And the scientist says, "We believe it's important that we focus on what we're *going* to do, not what we could do."

Now, that may sound like an absurd response. But you have to remember, we *did* know about climate change in the 1970s. And we *had* time to create a different world from the one we ended up with.

Just like we *have* time right now.

These technologies are in their infancy. And we have the time and the power *right now* to not only prevent the worst from happening, but to positively alter our day-to-day existence in a radical way.

And yet I hear expert after expert lining up to inform us as to the limits of our political will.
In other words, "We believe it's important that we focus on what we're *going* to do, not what we could do."

(Let us pray.)

You
are not capitalism.

(Amen?)

(Amen.)

The option that has been bought for you
When people say the political will isn't there for this kind of radical vision, what they're really saying is that these plans don't fit nicely within our current economic landscape.

If our futurists can't see more than a couple steps ahead due to the capitalist lens they must look through, how is the average person expected to radicalize around an alternative economic vision based on the promise of this emergent science?

You simply cannot talk about political will unless you talk about capitalism. And capitalism simply does not nurture *this kind* of political will.

And if we're honest about it, it has been a long long time since political will has had anything to do with the hopes and desires of the average person.
In today's world, political will is a matter of economic bargaining power.

Political will is not a matter of what *you* will choose.
It's a matter of what has been chosen *for* you. It is the option that has been bought for you.

In other words, it's not about what we *could* do.
It's about what we're going to do.

(Let us pray.)

Why commit to capitalism?
Why not commit to *us*?

You
are not capitalism.

(Amen?)

(Amen.)

But can I get rich

So let's step back from all the parables and analogies and grand talk for just a moment, and let's be clear about something.

The biggest problem with all this is *not* would it work. The biggest problem is that question in the back of everyone's mind.

Because, see, it wouldn't matter if the vision for our salvation was some one-in-a-million longshot or if aliens just showed up and gave it to us as a gift. The same five words would be in the back of everyone's mind.

"But can I get rich?"

You know it's true.
Just imagine if Martians came to Earth next week with an environmentally sustainable economic blueprint that ensured not one person would ever go without clothing, food, shelter, sanitation, education, and healthcare, that everyone in the world would have all their necessities met, in addition to a reasonable share of luxuries.

The first words out of our mouths wouldn't be "thank you" or "how would that work" or "when can we begin".
Our first words would be: "But can I get rich?"

And of course the Martians would have to explain to us that great disparity in resource allocation would simply not be compatible with their design.

And then we'd be like, "Oh, ok, I just wanted to make sure I understood you correctly: You're saying that your blueprint would basically guarantee every man, woman, and child on the planet a middle class lifestyle, but no one could ever be rich?"

And the Martian says, "Yes. That's exactly right."

And then we would say, after a really long pause of deep consideration, "Get the fuck out of here. I got your blueprint *right here.*"

You know that shit is true.

Go out in the street right now and ask the first person you come across.

"Excuse me, sir, I'd like to ask you a question. If we could eliminate hunger and preventable disease worldwide, but you couldn't ever get rich, would you do it?"

"Well, I mean that sounds really good… That sounds really good... But I don't know. I don't know about *not ever* getting rich. I mean what if I got so rich I could actually save all those people? Would that be ok?"

(EERRRRRRRRRRRR - Try again.)

"Ok, sir, well what about human trafficking? Would you sacrifice the possibility of riches to end human trafficking?"

"Oh, man. Human Trafficking? I mean I know that's some really bad stuff... But couldn't I get just a little rich?"
(EERRRRRRRRRRRR - Try again.)

"Ok, sir, then what about war?"

"Wait now, hold on, hold on. I know that war is bad. But you can't deny that there are also some good things that come out of war... You know, like... people getting rich."
(EERRRRRRRRRRRRRRRRRRRRRRRR)

You know that's how we think. It's who we are.

And here's the thing. *You* ain't never gonna be rich. You ain't neeeeever gonna be rich. If your ass ain't rich right now, you ain't never gonna be rich.

And yet I know what some of you are thinking right now.

"But I could be."

We're like the guy who gets lucky enough to find everything he's ever looked for in a partner, but he leaves her at the altar because he just realized if he gets married he'll never be able to have a three-way with supermodels.

That's who we are.

And that's why we've got to rethink all of this shit. We've got to rethink the concept of getting rich, or what it even means to be rich.

There are other byproducts
People act like becoming rich is the *only* byproduct of capitalism. When, in reality, it's just one byproduct, and an unlikely one at that. But there are other byproducts, many of which are quite horrific, almost all of which are more likely than you becoming rich.

Think about it. Just because a few can benefit from a system doesn't mean it is a good system. History is full of awful examples where a handful of people had good lives as a result of an utterly horrendous system. That is a low bar for accepting the morality of an economy.

If we plan on having a truly better world, we're going to have to make getting rich seem like a foreign concept, a silly concept, perhaps even an abhorrent concept. More of an antiquated shame, similar to the way we now think of slavery. And for those who think that is an unfair analogy, remember there was only a relative handful of economic big winners in that system, while masses suffered from it. The degree of suffering may be different, but the arguments of people benefitting from that system were the same back then as what is being said to justify capitalism's ills right now.

We need to rethink these concepts.
We don't need to think in terms of *getting* rich; we need to think in terms of *being* rich.

Because, a better world doesn't mean that no one can be rich. A better world means that we have a new definition of what it *means* to be rich. I would suggest that a better world is one in which everyone is rich.

So what does it mean to *be* rich?

You really want to know?

Go ask someone with stage four colon cancer what it would mean to be rich.
They will tell you that good health and access to good healthcare is wealth.

Go ask someone working in a sweatshop or a rose mill what it would mean to be rich.
They will tell you that human dignity and a fair share of the fruit of one's labor and the opportunity to find one's own true potential is wealth.

Go ask someone who lost their child to war. Ask them if they would rather have their child back or a sack full of money.
They will tell you that peace is wealth.
They will tell you that justice is wealth.
They will tell you that that child alive and breathing and laughing in their arms was wealth.

No, the only *getting* rich we need to think about is the journey we make to get to that better world, the steps it takes for us to eliminate our hardships and our drudgeries, to eliminate our injustices. And to do it for us all. That's what *getting* rich should mean.

Rethinking currency

Now, I believe it would be much easier to rethink our definition of being rich if we didn't have money. Therefore, I propose we set out to formally expunge the presence of money from the definition of being rich.

Not by ignoring the concept of money. But by making it disappear. By getting rid of it.

And I don't mean abolishing money. For you do not need abolition if you have obsolescence.

I believe we need to make money obsolete.

Part of going beyond capitalism is seeing *past* money. It's about imagining what a currency-less society might look like. And ultimately it's about envisioning what real efficiency might look like.
Because I believe even the couple of seconds it takes to dig your wallet out of your pocket or purse is a waste of time. Never mind the

accumulated amount of time we waste looking at a price tag and then trying to decide if we can afford to pay that price.

Pretty soon we're going to see software performing macro *and micro* budgeting that is so fast and accurate, that to even think in terms of price will be an exercise in gross inefficiency.

Yet it is not just about building that technology; it is about steering the technology. It's about us changing our lens.

In order to properly design or envision such technology, we have to start looking at goods in a different light.

For instance, price is perceived in individual terms. In other words, what do *I* have to sacrifice to have this?

Cost, on the other hand, can factor in what *everyone else* has to sacrifice in order for you to have this.

Instead of thinking in terms of "what is the price," we need to think in terms of "what is the cost."

If we are to have both a just *and efficient* society, our concept of cost must be expanded and our concept of monetary price must be made foreign.

And once we have accomplished this, once we have exposed how arbitrary and inefficient is our current incarnation of individual price, it will be a whole hell of a lot easier to prove currency obsolete.

Rethinking work and compensation

Of course, I can just hear the experts scoffing at how downright naive I am to even make such a suggestion. That, in fact, I have it backwards. The current trend with cryptocurrencies is an explosion of new currencies. Some predict that we might eventually see millions of currencies.

And that may very well be. But I don't believe that necessarily precludes my vision from taking hold. In fact, if we do see a future where there are literally millions of currencies, the definition of currency itself will have already been redefined and possibly even made irrelevant as it pertains to the actual economy.

And just like a lesson given to a child may seem different once they've grown older, I think our current cryptocurrency gurus will eventually come to see that Satoshi Nakamoto's gift of Bitcoin was the technological Trojan Horse that led to the obsolescence of currency itself.

We don't need to abolish money. The blockchain is going to help us create a system that no longer needs it.

Because the truth is we don't need it.

I think of currency merely as capitalism's flag. In that, a flag is nothing more than a piece of colored cloth. Its significance is derived from the story we are told about it.

And just like our demagogues tell us that the proof of our patriotism is in the number of flags we fly, capitalists tell us that economic health is measured in part by the circulation of currency throughout our economy.

In other words, it is your patriotic duty to spend money. And because you cannot spend money unless you have money, it is also your patriotic duty to make money. The moral of the story being that a life devoted to making and spending money is a life in service to the greater good.

And yet *what if* that story is fiction?

What if we're wrong?
What if it doesn't have to be this way?

Just think about how much of ourselves we sacrifice to affirm that story, how much bullshit we put up with to affirm that story.

What if we're just circulating money for the sake of circulating money?
What if we're killing ourselves at a job we can barely tolerate in the service of a misunderstanding?

What if making a living is really just running in place because we think if we stop moving we're going to die?
What if we are wrong?

Who gains from this story?

Well, I'll tell you who gains from this story.
Rich motherfuckers.

And yet who circulates the most currency?
Not rich motherfuckers.

It's like your boss making busy work for *you* to justify *their* salary.

Well, fuck that shit.
You can stick that story up your ass.

We have to rethink the concept of making a living.
We have to rethink the whole concept of income.

And part of rethinking the concept of income is *thinking* about the value of work.
Or should I say what *kind* of work is valued.

Meaning, first off, in a good economy, nobody gets a damn thing for doing work that isn't collectively valued.

I'm sure Wall Street motherfuckers work really hard at setting economic booby traps for our asses. It doesn't mean they should get compensated for it.

You got motherfuckers today making a hundred times what the average laborer makes for work that is actually antithetical to survival on the planet.

Well, fuck that shit!

You can work as much as you want to. If that work is unnecessary or counterproductive, you ain't getting shit.

You have the right to be compensated for valuable work, but the degree of that value *and the control over that value* is not an individual right.

Secondly, in a just and rational world, the person doing the shit work makes the most.

Granted, the goal is to have a well-educated population who do mostly fulfilling work, and what shit work is left should be spread out equitably so no one is doing too much of it. Not to mention, there's going to be less work to do overall as a result of automation and machine learning.

Nevertheless, if there are still some really dirty jobs left and somebody's *gotta* do 'em, those somebodies ought to be compensated proportionally.

If you're sloshing around in a sewer all day or sweating your ass off next to an industrial furnace, I personally believe you ought to get more than the person working on a cure for cancer.

Of course, you know what they're going to say to that: "Then why would anybody work on finding a cure for cancer?"

I don't know, maybe because finding a cure for cancer is fucking awesome.

There are different types of compensation.
Achievement is a reward.
Fame is a reward.
The challenge itself is a reward.
Making a contribution is a fucking reward.

We have to go from an economy of making a living to an economy of making a contribution.
Just like we have to go from competing against one another to competing against our own potential.

An economy of making a living ultimately pits you against others trying to make a living. It pits us against one another for our very survival.

Just think about that shit.
How are we ok with that shit?
Fuck... that shit.

We need to move from the concept of individual competition to the concept of collaborative competition, where the focus is more on collective record breaking and an achievement model that measures its success on how much it benefits everyone.

All winners. No losers. That's the goddamn goal.
And we have a real chance at that shit.
The question is: How attached are we to this flag?
Are we willing to question the story we've been told?
Are we willing to rethink and call out what's really going on in that story?
And are we courageous enough, audacious enough, to try and write a new one?

(Hallelujah!?!)

(Hallelujah.)

Anti-sermon 04
An Offering of Salvation (Part Two):
Some Real Motherfuckers

Rethinking Markets: In Algorithms We Trust

Are we courageous enough, audacious enough, to try and write a new story?
Because when we're talking about capitalism, we are primarily telling a story about who owns shit and how shit moves throughout the economy.

In other words, property and markets.

And when it comes to rewriting our economic story, these two are some real motherfuckers. In future economic narrative after future economic narrative, people have had a *really* hard time trying to rethink property and markets.

One might call it an epidemic of nearsightedness. And though the epidemic was not unavoidable, the nearsightedness itself is not altogether groundless, seeing that only recently have we birthed these new technologies and there *is* quite a bit of unearthing yet to do in regard to their potential.

Now, before we get to the nuances of what's mine and what's yours, or what should be owned at all, I want to talk a little about markets.

I personally believe markets are immoral, but I understand morality is subjective. And when you become an economist and start making six figures plus a year, it becomes even more subjective.

So, for the sake of urgency, I am willing to play on economists' turf and focus once again on the virtue of efficiency. For I believe there are no serious economists who can argue with a straight face that markets will not prove incredibly inefficient next to the coming technological alternatives.

Seriously, this new technology is going to make our concept of a market look fucking ridiculous. Every time you pick an item up off the grocery store shelf, look at the price, read the nutrition facts, and then try to calculate whether it makes sense to buy it, that process is completely inefficient.

In fact, negotiating a price for almost any individual transaction is absurd. Our comprehension, or rather our cerebral computing power, is simply not advanced enough to factor in all the relevant data (even if it was available to us - which it isn't) to make these kinds of decisions on a scale that is even close to as efficient as when performed by algorithmic software. It's a waste of time even trying.

Rethinking our economy boils down to *thinking* about the wisest use of resources and the efficiency of their allocation.

And no matter what you think about them today or yesterday, in tomorrow's technological landscape, markets are going to prove simply inefficient.

"But what about competition, what about competition?"

Well, for those who think competition is somehow a virtue, is it a greater virtue than efficiency? Because the moment you interject the element of competition, where one side wins at the expense of the other side losing (even if they both *think* it is mutually beneficial), you've corrupted the efficiency of the entire allocation process. You don't *have* to look at it as morality. It's a matter of efficiency.

And, look, you can still portray markets as Farmer Dave and Farmer Janet having the *liberty* to negotiate a price between themselves. And that may sound quite harmless, though I would argue *even that* is far less efficient than what I'm describing. But the reality of the market is that the negotiations are not between Farmer Dave and Farmer Janet; they're between Farmer Dave and Farmer Monsanto.

As long as you have competition, as long as you have the capacity for people to accumulate wealth or power at the expense of others, there will be people or groups of people who work relentlessly to chip away at all the gains you've made. And if you still don't want to look at *that* in terms of morality, you do have to look at it in terms of efficiency.

The processing speed of our machines and the sophistication of these algorithms will allow us to do away with competition, to do away with our highly fallible and often shortsighted decision-making ability, to do away with all this wasted time.

Now, that doesn't mean we don't have a say. The point of all this is that we *can* input what we want (our needs, our desires) in addition to all the other information *we* usually *don't* take into consideration. In other words, we can program in our values and our principles as it pertains to labor and manufacturing conditions, risks to the environment, and the abundance of raw materials and resources.

We're going to be able to do that shit. And the computations are going to be instantaneous.

Everything they said that the Invisible Hand of the Market would do but didn't? Well, this could actually do it. Except this isn't about faith. In fact, the Invisible Hand of the Algorithm isn't really invisible. It's transparent, or at least it can be. Meaning we can *all* have the power to guide it. Which ultimately means we all have the power to build an economy that is not only efficient but moral as well.
Think about it. Why in the fuck are we competing against one another? Let the algorithm figure that shit out.

Of course, a lot of folks are not yet ready to make the pledge "In Algorithms We Trust." They just can't get comfortable with the idea of an algorithm economy.

But goddamn! Don't we already live in an algorithm-based economy? It's called capitalism. That's what the system is. It's an *organic* algorithm based on certain assumptions of how things are or should be done. The implicit biases, conventional wisdom, and established precedent that have consistently put profits over people and made corporations *into* people are really no more than factors in an equation.

Well, guess what? We can make a new equation. One that *is* transparent. One that *is* accountable. And if it turns out not to be a perfect equation, we can *remake* it. Again and again.

These algorithms are not deities dictating what we do and how we do it. They're not some new creator we have to bow down and worship. They're *our* creations. They are shaped and reshaped by us.

But that's just it. We have to be there to shape them. We have to show up. We have to be a part. And we have to be open to rethinking not only markets, but rethinking everything.

Because it's not just about goods and services. We have to rethink how we allocate our social contracts, how we allocate our political desires. We have to rethink the mechanisms of democracy itself.

And that means no political markets either. Seriously, y'all. That ritual we perform every couple years where we choose which stranger to surrender our voice to, our power to? That thing we call voting? Well, that shit is horse and buggy.

Why in the hell do allow a bunch of out of touch ignoramuses to make decisions about *our* healthcare or *our* communications? Why are we trusting a cabal of corrupt donor-boners to make binding policy on water safety, air pollution, and fucking climate change? The shit makes no sense.

Very soon, we're going to be able to design and implement smart legislation, where policy is swiftly but flexibly enacted based on the values and principles of the people *most impacted* by each given policy.

See, I *dream* of the day when my grandkids can look back at our dumbasses and shake their heads at how inefficient and backwards shit used to be. Not just because I believe a better world would require an upgraded version of democracy, but more so because I believe if we don't hurry up and get off this electoral horse and buggy, my grandkids will actually be looking back at what little democracy we had and wondering how they can get *that* shit back.

Rethinking Property

Now, even if you can get down with the idea that we are eventually going to develop algorithms powerful enough to replace markets of all kinds, even if you can get down with the idea that those algorithms will produce a more desirable outcome, there's still a question in the back of everyone's mind. Except this time, it's a different five words.

"Who owns all my shit?"

If there's no price because there's no currency, and you can't really buy shit the same way you did before, can you still own shit?

Of course, before answering that question, it is important to point out, fuck that question.

That's not the question you should be asking. The question you should be asking is: Is owning shit necessarily a good thing?

I mean if we're really going to rethink our economic institutions, it's going to require us taking a long look at our concept of property.

I know we've been led to believe that more is better, but I would contend that owning less is better.

Think about it. If there are less things for people to individually own, there are obviously less things we have to produce, requiring less of our planetary resources, requiring less of our labor resources, ultimately producing the leftover byproduct of free time, as in free time for us to do whatever the fuck we want to do (except go shopping).

Now, that doesn't mean you can't own anything. Let me say that again. This does not mean you cannot own anything. It just means we have to interrogate and narrow down what are the things we absolutely *have to* possess.

When you factor in how much could be stored and made readily available and/or deliverable through neighborhood goods libraries, there's very little you actually *have to* own.

When you factor in the autonomous software that will soon be a part of everything from transportation to living spaces, there's very little you *have to* individually possess.

I believe, in a better world, most actual ownership will fit into the category of the sentimental, and a good deal of that will be suitable for digital capture.

And it's not just about the greater efficiency offered in this vision of a better world. We need to move to a transparent and truly democratic temporary-use society because the status quo on property relations is not only unsustainable, it is a future fucking catastrophe.

Because while we're over here pondering whether or not we can own our favorite teddy bear, what we should be pondering is: Who owns the algorithm?
Who owns the robots?
Who owns the brains inside the goddamn robots?
Who owns all *that* shit?

And the answer had better be *all* of us.

As long as this technology is open and decentralized, it will be incompatible with the status quo. But that is some shit that has to get settled.

Because *unless* this technology is open and decentralized, it will most definitely be bogarted and co-opted and frankensteined into something too fucked up for *Black Mirror*.

I personally believe that's a very *real* possibility and that we're going to have to fight like hell against that possibility. Yet in order to be effective in that fight, we have to have a clear understanding of what it is we're fighting for.

And again, that takes rethinking some big fucking concepts.

Because, see, the most important question concerning property is not who owns your knick-knacks or your sentimental treasures. It's not who owns the machinery or the factories or even the raw materials and fuel sources. It's not who owns the physical property. The most important question is who owns the *intellectual* property.

Rethinking Intellectual Property: Digging upward/forward

And before we even get into who should *own* this so-called intellectual property, we should first ask, "What is intellectual property?"

Well, it's the concept that you can own knowledge, or at least a particular expression of knowledge. We'll call it a piece of knowledge.

So what does it mean to own a piece of knowledge?

Well, it means you have control over what *can't* be done with that piece of knowledge.

You'll notice that I didn't use the word can. And that's because without knowledge being controlled, anything *can* be done with it. Ownership is about what cannot be done with it.

And that control over what cannot be done is so important to us that we consider it a right. A right that must be protected.

And what does it mean to protect intellectual property?

Well, it could mean a lot of things. It could mean stopping some jerk from cutting you out of the fortune they made by singing a song that you wrote. Something that, to the songwriter, is very serious. But far more serious than that, not to mention more serious to far more people, protecting intellectual property *could* mean making sure an important piece of technology never sees the light of day.

And it doesn't matter whether it's the inventor that denies society the benefit of this technological breakthrough or if the inventor sells it to a company with the same intentions.

In this system, it's not the knowledge that matters.
It's not the progress that matters.
It's the ownership that matters.

It's control that matters.

The concept of intellectual property is about protecting a system of control.

Protecting the knowledge of a lifesaving drug *could* mean keeping it a secret, preventing it from ever being produced.

And yet we consider that a right.

The knowledge would still exist. It just can't exist on our terms, only on the owner's terms.

Treating a piece of knowledge as property is nothing more than granting the right to decide who will not benefit from it, even if that benefit is the saving of one's life.

Because, see, in this system it's not *really* about protecting the knowledge.
It's about protecting control.

But why?
Why would we protect an *owner's right* to control a lifesaving drug before we protect the life of someone who needs that drug?

Why does anyone deserve that kind of control?
For that matter, why does any one individual deserve control at all?

If we're willing to treat these pieces of knowledge like anything else that can be owned in the physical world, we have to acknowledge that they exist. Meaning they exist whether we own them or not.
Meaning they exist whether we discover them or not.

Furthermore, what does it even mean to discover something?

Just like the tired myth of the self-made millionaire, I think it's important we rethink our concept of the inventor.

Why do we give the inventor that kind of power?
Moreover, why would we trust them with that kind of power?

Is the kind of control we afford ownership really just about *being first*?

Can we really assume being first to figure something out means you will make the best decision for its use?
Is being first worth being able to deny the rest of humanity the potential benefit of that discovery?

Is that what we're saying? Are these people *that* special?

Or does this kind of control, this kind of rightful ownership, derive from the idea that this new thing would have never existed without you, and only you?

Is that what we're saying? Are these people *that* special?

Certainly not. The history of invention has proven that almost every major breakthrough was only a few days or weeks ahead of its discovery by someone else halfway across the world.

Furthermore, each teacher that inspired you to do better, each book you read that changed your perspective, each conversation you had that gave you insight, each of these is partially responsible for that "invention."

The roads to get back and forth to your library, to your school, to your laboratory. The devices and infrastructure you used to communicate with colleagues. The wealth of other inventions that had to come before this one *could* be discovered. Those are all partially responsible for your invention/breakthrough.

And yet with the kind of praise we heap on your asses, you would think you were raised by wolves and then somehow figured out time travel.

It's not enough that you found a gold watch on the beach, we have to act like you also invented the metal detector.

When in reality, your ass is metal detecting in a treasure chest, and the metal detector is just the accumulation of contributions that made up your life experiences.

All our foundational knowledge is like a treasure map. It's like a treasure map inside of the previous treasure chest.

It's all just layers of excavation, unearthing what is possible.

We need to think of inventors as archaeologists of the future. Instead of digging downward, they're digging upward.

In traditional archaeology, you might get excited to find a primitive tool to help you explain the past. Well, I like to think of our scientists and researchers as uncovering future tools. And the excitement is not just that they uncovered them; it's the hints they give us toward explaining what the even more distant future might look like.

Whether it is science or art, we need to think of the pursuit of knowledge as if we were excavating the ceiling of a cave, again digging upward. Where each new something found will ultimately add to that which we stand upon, allowing us to reach a little higher and find the next something.

Just remember, these somethings already exist. They are there, waiting for us to remove another layer of dirt.

That's why intellectual property is so ridiculous. It's like treating something you dug up as if it were your creation.

When in reality we're all just stumbling upon what was already there, what already exists.

And whether by intention or by accident, being the first person to stumble upon something doesn't make it any more yours than calling "shotgun infinity" is a legally binding contract to sit in the front seat for the rest of time.

The real problem is not who's going to get there first.
The real problem is that there is so much digging to do, and so many different places to dig.

That's why it's better to have a coordinated effort, where information is shared and efforts are not stifled by the secrets demanded by greed and competition.

That's why I say fuck competition.
And fuck greed.
And fuck intellectual property.

There's too much important shit buried out there for you to be hoarding your portion of the goddamn treasure map. Because the truth is, if we don't find the right place to dig, that earth-shaking, future-changing, species-saving breakthrough could just as easily stay undiscovered forever.

So I'm not telling those already out there digging to quit digging.
I understand that, to find shit, we have to dig.

I'm just suggesting we rethink how we dig, and why it is we're digging.
Otherwise, we may not have that much time left to dig.
You dig?

From Banksy to Satoshi Nakamoto: Anonymity and a Fame Economy

"But where's the incentive?"
Isn't that what people always ask when you talk about a more progressive allocation of wealth and resources? Where's the incentive?

If there's no market and there's no money, that means there's no big paycheck for inventors to look forward to.

And if there's no pot of gold waiting at the end of the creative or scientific rainbow, why would anyone create?
Where's the incentive?
Where's the compensation?

Well, the hopes are, once we've moved from a making a living economy to a making a contribution economy, just knowing that you've made that contribution would be enough.

But if you still need something that is yours and only yours, you still need to have more than others have, if there's still some selfish and greedy tendencies left in you, you can rest easy knowing that we have a little something left over from the bad old days.

And that is fame.
And fame is some big shit.

You can be a trillionaire and drop the fuck dead tomorrow. But fame doesn't have to die.
The old saying about money is, "you can't take it with you." But with fame, you can sure as fuck leave it here.

(Hallelujah!?!)

(Hallelujah.)

Now, some might not be all that comfortable with the idea of vanity as currency, but I believe fame will prove quite useful, especially as our perspective on fame evolves.

I personally hope we will see less striving for individual fame and more working together in pursuit of collective fame, similar to the pride that comes along with being part of a group or a team. Except, in this case, the team doesn't win just for themselves. They win for everyone. And by making fame about a collective effort to benefit everyone else, it is ultimately about making a contribution.

Now, I'm not naive enough to believe that individual fame is going to simply go away. Nor should it. There's lots of great work to be done on our own. In fact, some of the most important steps in our revolution may require work that is done completely alone.

To get us to a making a contribution economy, we're going to have to commit to a number of strategic peccadilloes. Some of which are going to be so antithetical to the status quo, they're going to have to be performed anonymously.

That's why, not only do I believe people will eventually embrace the incentive of fame over the incentive of making more money than they can spend, I believe that along the way you're going to see a new kind of fame emerge.

Because, see, anonymity offers another element to fame.

Satoshi Nakamoto has become the Banksy of Money, or as I prefer - the future Zodiac Killer of Capitalism. It's not just the contribution; it's the intrigue of not knowing who that person is.

Similarly, avatar activism offers a chance not just at fame, but at legend.

Yet no matter how large that legend gets, if no one else knows it's you, then it ultimately is about the contribution.

And if all this talk about a fame economy and upward/forward excavation is a little too on the philosophical side for you, well, too fucking bad. We need philosophy right now. We need perspective right now. We need the mental tools to be able to make the most of these new scientific tools.

And while I may be lingering in the philosophical, and I may be focusing on the future, this isn't some imaginary shit.

The day before I wrote this part of the sermon, I turned on the radio and heard yet another American economist being interviewed about China and the "theft" of our intellectual property. And it got me to thinking that, in a better world, they would simply be talking about folks in China making the most out of our intellectual contribution, in turn making said contribution that much greater.

The problem is not the theft of intellectual property.
The problem is intellectual property.
If anything, intellectual property is the greatest theft of all.

How we share each step
(Let us pray.)

Proudhon wrote
that property is theft.
This most certainly includes
intellectual property.

Intellectual property robs
those after you
and those before you.

For each work is a link
in the chain of what is possible.

And treating that link
as property
is a theft of what is possible.
It is a theft of potential.
It is about what *cannot* be done.

By "protecting" your "property"
you rob yourself
of real potential.

And if we really believe
we can do better
than the world we are currently inhabiting
we have to quit robbing ourselves
of our potential.

These new tools must be accompanied

by a new way of thinking.
How we use what we have.
How we go about finding
what we do not yet have.
And how we share each step
that gets us there.

(Amen?)

(Amen.)

Stumbled upon

A few years ago, I listened to an interview with the founder of one of these fake meat companies. And he talked about how a cow's stomach was really just a machine that could turn grass into protein. And that he wanted to understand that process to the degree that he could replicate it with actual machinery. And that once the replication process was perfected, you wouldn't be able to tell the difference between his so-called fake beef and the beef we've been used to eating our whole lives. Because, at that point, there would be no real difference.

And it got me to thinking *if* that would be enough. If they could sustainably and affordably mass produce a substance with a taste, a texture, and nutritional offering identical to the contents of an old-fashioned hamburger, how many people would still want to keep the slaughterhouses running merely for the sake of nostalgia?

For thousands of years, humans believed that plants had to come from the ground.
And why? Because that's how we stumbled upon them.

For even longer, humans thought the only way to reproduce was through intercourse.
And why? Because that's how we stumbled upon it.

Obviously, things are a bit different today. We have fertility clinics and reproductive research labs. We have aquaponics and all manner of indoor farming.

And yet how many have resisted these breakthroughs out of some sort of irrational attachment for the way things used to be?
How many feel that embracing the science is somehow rejecting the world as they have come to know it?

Of course, it isn't the world that has changed.
It is our understanding of the world that has changed.
And the moment we were willing to look beneath the surface and gamble that there might be something more than what we had originally stumbled upon, *we* changed.

And that is a good thing. A very good thing.

Whether it is sentimentality or superstition, we cannot let romanticization keep us from the benefits of the physical world.
Especially when harnessing these insights could mean saving the world.

Now, that doesn't mean there are no ethical concerns with the science and/or the implementation of that science. There are.

Because, see, it's not just meat we are rethinking.

Pretty soon, we may see intelligence and consciousness in a completely different light.
We may rethink the very concept of evolution; we may redefine what it means to be human.
And one day, it may be time and matter we are recognizing that we only stumbled upon.

That is precisely why our curiosity must extend beyond just the field of science.
The principles and values that go into making these kinds of decisions, these ethical judgment calls, don't come out of just one sphere of influence; they come out of all our social spheres.

There is more than the religion we found ourselves in.
There is more than the family relations we grew up in.
There is more than the schools that have both fed and filtered our potential.
There is more than the workplaces we have permitted to justify our existence.
There is more than the civic structures that make us believe we must be governed.
There is more than the economy for which we are told there is no alternative.

We must be willing to go beyond that world.
We must be unafraid to question what more is possible.

A better world is more than how much we know about the physical world. It is what we do with what we know, and why.

We cannot let convention smother our imagination.
Nor can we let the familiar serve as shelter from the unknown.

We must listen for what the future is whispering to us.

Even if it means breaking from our victories, even if it means departing from the paths of resistance that got us this far, we must critically embrace new ways of thinking and seeing, we must take up the courage of real imagination, and we must be ready to gamble on something different.

There are different worlds. We have stumbled upon this one.

Anti-sermon 05
A Call to the Altar (Part One):
Whatever It Takes

No center, no trust, no permission.
(Let us pray.)

This
is what we've been waiting for.

Better yet
it's what they've been telling us
to wait for

because they never thought
it was possible.

Nonviolence.

No center. No trust. No permission.
An almost perfect resistance.

There will be no one to attack.
No one to smear.
No one to set up.
No one to visit in the night.

The thing will just exist.

And once it exists
it can't unexist.

This is not to say
that the genie cannot
be put back in the bottle.

It is to say
our first job will be

to smash all the bottles.

(Amen?)

(Amen.)

What are you going to do?
Years ago, at the Climate Forum in Copenhagen, I listened to an activist from Northeast India describe the perils of her region. It was only 2009 and, in the midst of their own crisis, they were already experiencing climate refugees coming in from places that had it even worse.

She then paused to look at each of the Western activists sitting around her.

She asked them, "What are you going to do?"

They answered, "Everything we can."

She replied, "No.
That is the wrong answer.
You've already been doing that.

You must do
whatever it takes."

I think about that a lot.
I think about how long people have been doing everything they can.
And somehow we still haven't found a home for justice.

If we are to win a better world, we are going to have to do - whatever it takes.
Lucky for us, we now have what it takes.

When we recognize that
(Let us pray.)

It's not the data or the algorithms.
It's not the sensors or the networking of devices.
It's not the automation or the open source production.
It's not the machine learning, the artificial intelligence.

It's the catalyst.
It's what allows all of these to be used, to be combined, in a way that would otherwise be impossible.

It's what allows us to do what we could never do before.

Time-stamped. Transparent.
Distributed. Unowned.
Trustless. Open.
Permissionless. Powerful.

If we can shepherd the reaction, if we can harness this catalyst,
we have a shot at revolution.

Not in the sense that a better world is now possible.
A better world was always possible.

The revolution is the possibility of all this being accomplished nonviolently.
That's what the blockchain offers.

But only if we acknowledge.
What makes the blockchain strong is what makes us strong.

Numbers
in unity.

Connected
and working together.

Equitably.

A lasting solidarity.
That is what the blockchain offers.

When we recognize that
we will recognize our future.

(Amen?)

(Amen.)

We need you in the room

Of course, the technology is not our savior. But neither are we as individuals. It's not one person; it's *each* person. Each person doing their part.

And I want to emphasize something here. We still need the folks in the streets. We still need folks agitating to correct injustices. A revolution absent an organized fight against racism, sexism, homophobia, classism, imperialism, and all other hierarchical oppressions is not a revolution. These societal ills nurture the very future we fear. And if we are to make this technology a tool for real progress, we are going to need protesters just as much as we need programmers.

Having said that, I don't want to make it sound as if those who are not in the streets have no place in protest. Quite the contrary, I believe you can find a way to contribute from even the most privileged positions. But we should be honest about that privilege. It is a debt, and one that we have to make good on.

If you are not in a place where you are *actively* seeking justice for the oppressed, then you must find a place to *actively* seek a future free from oppression.

Now, that may sound quite daunting. But remember, the future is pretty big, and so is this revolution. There is space for you in it.

If we are to free ourselves from the bondage of private ownership over productive property, we *need* people to help develop open source automation that compliments open source hardware.

If we are to even approach the concept of post-scarcity and realize a *real* sharing economy, we *need* people to help develop a far more efficient recycling process. For goods, for packaging, for everything.

If we are to finally achieve equity in employment and an employment allocation mechanism free from the bargaining power of knowledge base, we *need* people to help develop neuro-tech that allows for speed learning of skills and trades, for ultra-speed learning of formulas, processes, and design.

Certainly, these types of technologies are in the works. But it matters who is in the room when and where they are being developed. We need someone with our values in that room.

You don't put sexist pigs in charge of women's magazines, and you don't leave amoral capitalism in charge of the algorithms.

Just like those who enlisted during the War against Vietnam to organize from within, we need people to go undercover in the laboratory where they design the future.

Whether it's entrepreneurs or researchers or worker bees, we need you in that room.

Now, this doesn't mean everyone already in the room is nefarious. But it also doesn't mean they're neutral. Anyone who thinks they're not inputting their own bias in the mix ignores the bias our system has already instilled in us.

And it's not even that we want a room free from bias. It's that we want to choose the bias. We want a bias against injustice, against inequity, and toward humanity.

But in order to have that, we have to be in the room.

And in order to increase our odds of having the right ideas in the right place at the right time, we have to get a whole lot of people to rethink a whole lot of shit. Because there is a whole lot of shit that has to be done.

But that means there's space. There's space in this revolution. For assholes like me, and assholes like you.

The point is that you can get in where you fit in, but goddamn it you better get in.

Incitement to nonviolence: a public trial of our values

Now, I want to be up front about something.
I've come here today to incite.
Let me say that again: I've come here today to incite.
I've come here to incite nonviolence.

But maybe not for the reasons you might think.

Regardless of your moral stance on violent revolution, it must be acknowledged that we have come to a place where, no matter what we do, we simply cannot win the violence.

Winning a revolution today is winning the *nonviolence.*

Now, what does that mean?

Well, what it does *not* mean is that our path will be without deviation. Revolution by its very definition demands deviation.

The definition of revolution has not changed. The vehicle providing opportunity for deviation, however, has changed.

While, obviously, our actions can never be free from risk, encryption technology and identity protecting communication infrastructure may significantly reduce that risk.

The matter, at that point, is not whether actions are performed underground or above the cloud. The matter is how we justify them.

Reduced risk does not mean we abandon our principles. Quite the contrary, it charges us to put our principles in the spotlight.

In this new era of technology, we are going to see revolutionaries announce the actions before they happen. And I mean actual advertisements, laying out instructions on how to safely execute specific endeavors and transparently representing the strategic value of such actions. Open invitations to anyone who can grasp the gravity of the moment and who might just feel moved to participate.

This will not only allow potential perpetrators the opportunity to interrogate their convictions and decide what those convictions are worth to them, it will allow us all to hold public trial of our values.

Before we can take back the world, we must take back our minds. Each one of us must take back our conscience.

Who gave you your conscience?
Who gave you your principles?

I would argue that, for most of us, it is the system. The same system that keeps us from reaching our full potential, the same system we so often find ourselves cowering beneath, groveling beneath, withering beneath.

Do we owe that system our compliance?
Do we owe the people who maintain that system our compliance?

Or do we owe them deviation?

The only way we can win a nonviolent revolution is if we revolutionize nonviolence.

Each action, each step toward victory, will be an open conversation. One that demands participation, requires introspection, and illuminates our commitment.

By imploring the majority to commit, one way or the other, you gamble less on the efficacy of the actions and more on the legitimacy of their justification.

In other words, the gamble is not about defeating those in power. It's about winning the support of those without power.

Even then, it's not about winning the hearts and minds of the public. It's about getting the public to win their own.

Do we owe this system our compliance?
Or do we owe this system deviation?

Let this question stand as an incitement to nonviolence.
Let your answer be revolution.

(Hallelujah!?!)

(Hallelujah.)

INDIEnet

So let's talk about that deviation.

No matter what your take is on capitalism, the decentralization sought by so many in the blockchain world is, in a sense, a seizing of the means of production.

And while I believe decentralization is a big step in the right direction, I also believe it is not enough. For anything that can be seized can be seized back.

Moreover, what good is the seizing of warehouses and manufacturing plants if you do not have control over the roads?

If we are to avoid traditional legal battles, backdoor spying, and the threat of total shutdown, we must go beyond our current concept of decentralization.

Now, this doesn't mean we also seize the digital roadways. It means we build new ones.

It is not enough to overlay new software and protocols on existing communication infrastructure. We need our own infrastructure. Which means we need hardware.

We need an INDIEnet. We need to create, produce, and disseminate a mass grid of inexpensive, open source nodes that relay signal between themselves and a tiny accessory-like device/chip attached to our current smartphones. We need an INDIEnet.

This is not only possible, it is a necessity.

The blockchain can provide us a more democratic space for goods and service allocation.
The INDIEnet would allow for movement of those products and those services, movement that is truly free.

If we are to unleash the full potential of the blockchain, we need our own hardware infrastructure. We need the roads. We need an INDIEnet.

True decentralization of power is to de-own the means through which power functions.
True decentralization of the blockchain will require movement along an infrastructure that is un-ownable.

And that, ultimately, is *not* about seizing the means of production. It's about freeing it.
That is what an INDIEnet would do.

And that would be true deviation.

The Great Flood

Of course, building an INDIEnet is not just a technical deviation; it is an ideological deviation. I would suggest it is a moral deviation. Because when we talk about revolution, we're not just trying to find our way to a place with different technical norms. We're trying to find our way to a place with different ideological norms, indeed different moral norms.

One day, we will look back and see intellectual property as a sin. We will see the hiding of technology as a sin. We will see the hoarding of information as a sin. We will see the acquisition and confiscation of scientific research as a sin. We will see the denying of solutions, the denying of medicine, through patents as a sin. We will see the tribalization of our scholars as a sin. We will see the rationing of our access to and knowledge of the potential of the physical world, thus the rationing of our potential as human beings, as a sin. All in the name of competition. All in the name of profit. All in the name of a false idol, an economic fiction to which we have pledged our faith.

It is a sin. And we need something to wash away that sin. We need for something to come along and wash away that stain on our collective conscience.

Well, folks, I believe it is coming.

I believe very soon we are going to see something come along and wash it all away.
I believe very soon we are going to see a Great Flood.

A flood like no one has ever seen before.
A flood not of rain, but a flood of leaks.

For like a flash of lightning and a roar of thunder, a call will soon be handed down for knowledge to be freed from the bondage of property status and let flow into an open and distributed Commons.

And for 40 days and 40 nights, so-called intellectual property will come pouring in.

Except it will not fall from the sky. It will rise up from below, released by a million lone actors who hear this call and quietly answer.

I believe very soon we are going to see a Great Flood.

Yet I am not the only one who can see the coming of this flood.

Because, see, before the bottom drops out of our corporate skies, the patriarchs of this family will move to build a more perfect vault. An ark, if you will, to collect and keep "safe" all the 0s and 1s in the known world.

That is why it is so important that we ready ourselves for this flood. For, if we are to be redeemed, this flood must begin before they are able to finish building that ark, before they are able to fill it, and before they are able to close its doors forever.

And when this Great Flood is over, after those 40 days and 40 nights of sharing what was always ours, we can be sure there will be consequences. And that is why it is so important that this flood *must* be followed by a rainbow of discovery, a rainbow of innovation and collaboration, a rainbow of the stories, the moments, the memories rescued by greater access to scientific research and life-saving medicine.

And as that trial, that long overdue conversation, is being held, this rainbow will stand as a demonstration of why such a flood had to happen, as a reminder of why we heeded the call, and as a warning that if we do not ultimately wash away this sin of intellectual property, the next time it will be fire.

The Great Drought

Now, when we speak of liberation and the INDIEnet, when we speak of being washed clean by a Great Flood, what we're ultimately speaking about is the flow of data. And the way in which that flow is directed, manipulated, and/or controlled will determine which future we have either the pleasure or the shame of inhabiting.

So let's talk a little about that data.

Data is quickly becoming, or has already become, the most important currency there is. Unsurprisingly, it took little time for those who trade in this new currency to find their own way into predatory lending.

We cannot wait for capitalism to produce new tech companies big enough to take on the threats we face in this new Wild West of data, only then to pray that these *new corporations on the block* don't morph into something even worse. Fortunately, these silicon behemoths are susceptible to the same strategies of divestment as their Wall Street counterparts.

In other words, we must deprive them of their currency.

Imagine software that clones the functionality of these sites, cloaks our data, hides the ads, and then notifies advertisers that their ad dollars were spent in vain.

Or imagine software that strategically feeds the wrong data into their algorithms and feeds the right data into an alternative open source algorithm programmed to produce *real* value for that data's rightful owner.

Now imagine these things being done on the turf of an INDIEnet where the big boys don't have the means of law or policy enforcement.

Just imagine it.

Will it go down this way? I have no idea. I don't even know if it's technically possible. The point of the exercise is not to predict the future but to get the folks who could figure something like this out a tad more curious and/or hungry for the challenge.

Similar to the Great Flood of leaks, we need a Great Drought of data.

This does not mean we do away with data. It just means we take back access and control over what is ours, and in the process we dry up the very lifeblood that sustains these unaccountable, amoral mass communication juggernauts.

There is no rule that says algorithms have to be programmed, controlled, and owned by corporations. There's no rule that says these corporations have to exist.

These entities are just data and ads. Nothing more.

We already have the capability for data to be used on our terms, free from outside manipulation and with far greater efficiency.

If we can keep data private and strictly permission-based, we can make advertising irrelevant and the current business model obsolete.

If we can ensure that data is no longer a corporate currency, no longer the currency of robber barons, we reduce the risk of future wars being fought in that currency's name.

(Amen?)

(Amen.)

We give them a choice

Now, I understand that these ideas, these strategies, to the average person may seem a little too *out there*, just like the better world I am describing may seem a little too pie-in-the-sky. But that is the very nature of revolution. It is a break from what we have been socially conditioned and economically nurtured to perceive as desirable, as acceptable, as possible.

In the same vein, a lot of people believe that the idea of post-scarcity is simply pie-in-the-sky. I, on the other hand, believe if we wisely and efficiently utilize our technology, post-scarcity is a given.

I believe the only reason why it seems so fantastic is because in a post-scarcity world, there ain't no rich motherfuckers. And while we may have an idea of how to get to that place technologically, we have a harder time imagining how we get there culturally.

Wealth inequality has become a part of our culture the same as the glorification of violence. In fact, I would say the two are quite similar, in that they both paint savage competition as a natural order in the service of justifying humanity's greatest shames.

A better world is not a matter of technology. It's a matter of imagination and political will, kindled by an acknowledgment of where the status quo inevitably ends.

Machine learning is coming. More sophisticated and proliferative automation is coming.

If we are to avoid the trap of a Universal Basic Income Trojan Horse that ends up leaving us even more dependent on a corrupt system, we must begin a conversation that may at the start feel a tad uncomfortable.

Dismantling disproportionate power is a matter, in part, of dismantling wealth inequality. In other words, they're going to have to give some shit up.

I spoke before about not being able to *get* rich in a post-scarcity world. But what about those who are rich right now? What do we do with them?

Well, I'll tell you what we do. We give them a choice.

See, they know they have disproportionate power. They know they have disproportionate resources. Meaning they *could* facilitate our transition to a better world a lot faster and a lot smoother.

So I say we show them our blueprint. We show them what a better world would look like, and exactly how we can get there. We lay it all out on the table.

And then we give them the choice of getting on board. We give them the option to help make that shit happen. Otherwise, we make them publicly acknowledge their contentment with what business as usual has in store for us.

There are different futures to choose from. Unless these people are using their wealth to actively change this system in a fundamental way, they are coming for our future. Let me say that again. Unless they are actively working to, at the very least, reverse wealth inequality, they are already coming *for us.*

And if they make that choice, if they can be shown a world where everyone is afforded human dignity and reject that world because it does not afford obscene privilege, then our only option is to come *for them.*

Old men will tell you if you ever get cornered by a group of assholes and you know those assholes plan to do you harm, you single one of those assholes out and you attack him, quickly and brutally, giving the rest of those assholes something to think about. You leave an example and hope that they won't want to risk what is coming next.

While it is crucial that we address entire industries with different macro-strategy like the INDIEnet, The Great Flood, and the Great Drought, we're going to have to single one or two of these assholes out.

And we're going to have to do it in style.
Oh, yes, I'm talking sensational. Real dramatic-like.

First, we announce a draft of the worst actors within the Forbes 400 who have by that time publicly turned down our offer of finding their place in that better world. And then we hold an anti-lottery. Where if your number comes up, your ass just got poor.

But before that, we tell the world why you were in the draft to begin with. We tell the true story of how you got all that money, what you're currently doing to get more money, and worst of all how you invest that money politically. All at our expense.

And then we allow the *public* to deliver your reward. Think of it like a Robin Hood kickstarter, where we crowdsource suggestions on how to exact a little economic payback, and then we post online the best, most creative, nonviolent suggestions for folks to participate in.

Remember, we have the numbers. They have the money. If we can figure out a way to turn those numbers into power, they don't have the money anymore.

Now, I don't mean we have to ruin them. In fact, we can leave them a quite respectable living, the *same* as we expect.

The point is that if you take a motherfucker who's used to being rich and you make that motherfucker not rich, or even significantly less rich, and you do it *nonviolently*? Well, that is definitely going to give the rest of those rich motherfuckers something to think about.

I can just picture these wealthy assholes at home in their mansions, biting their nails as they tune in to the next anti-lottery, watching those little ping pong balls kick around the glass box, praying their number doesn't come up.

If you're not laughing your ass off, it almost makes you feel a little sorry for them. That is, until you remember the gravity of our choices up ahead and that the primary obstacles standing between us and a very different future that is *absolutely possible* are the motherfuckers occupying a societal status that should have been made obsolete a long long time ago.

And for anyone who would scoff at such a proposal, anyone who would describe such a proposal as naive, in other words, anyone who believes that it is *impossible* to correct this kind of wealth inequality through nonviolent means, through existing institutional means, then let *that* be your commitment to every other proposal I have made here. Let that stand as the ultimate justification for the new institutions we are calling for. Institutions that make their money irrelevant. Institutions that make their power irrelevant.

For as long as there are institutions that recognize and respect this kind of obscene wealth disparity, those institutions will recognize and respect the same kind of obscene power disparity. And you *know*, no matter what political language you speak, what that disparity translates to.

All of us, with open eyes and a conscience, acknowledge that. What other choice do we have but to try and breathe life into different institutions, to try and breathe life into a different world?

Nothing personal

Now, because *so many* people believe they're going to be rich one day, a good deal of folks tend to take this kind of talk personal. And, frankly, I don't give a fuck. Because, number one, your ass ain't never gonna be rich. Number two, going from rags to riches doesn't remedy the injustice of either. And number three, your ass ain't never gonna be rich.

What I *do* understand is if you take personal what I'm about to say, even though I am sincere when I tell you I do not want you to take it that way.

Nevertheless, I really *really* hope a lot of y'all are going to lose y'all's jobs. In fact, I'm going to try and make that happen.

Now, before you walk out on this entire sermon/revival, let me explain why I would say such a thing.

See, a lot of folks recognize that, in terms of our economic *machine*, the poor and working class are the fuel. What they often miss, however, is that the professional/managerial class is the oil.

Now, in order to stop the machine from running, you either take away the fuel or you take away the oil. Unfortunately, as long as this particular machine *is* running, there's always going to be a steady supply of poor people to consume and spit out. Meaning our only real chance at lasting change is to reduce the oil. In other words, we're going to have to find a way to shrink the number of people in the professional/managerial class willing to go along with business as usual, and then hope it is enough to bring the machine to a halt.

Ironically, as so many in the professional/managerial class watched *seemingly unbothered* as automation put more and more working class folks out of a job, nowadays it is the *oil* that is increasingly becoming synthetic.

Artificial intelligence and the reorganization of hierarchical communication are going to do away with the kinds of jobs the middle and upper middle class thought would last forever.

And that may not necessarily be a bad thing, especially if the pace of this per capita job loss surpasses that of the working class.

I personally believe a lot of the middle and upper middle class will get behind a Universal Basic Income when they see the number of working class jobs lost to automation. The problem is a Universal

Basic Income is not what's going to save us. We need something more than that, something different than that.

While often in favor of incremental reforms, *our* middle class has long stood in the way of radical change.

As long as they were untouched by the need for that change, they tethered human rights to the convenient and expected those without to consider them generous.

It is only when they see themselves as one day needing a Universal Basic Income, that their political imaginations may prove their elasticity.

It is only when they realize that so much more *is* possible, especially now that so little work is actually required by humans, that their definition of economic justice may expand.

It is only when they realize that the dissolving of *their* power, and thus their class, will only strengthen those at the very top, making everyone else below *even more* vulnerable, that their urgency to act may become demonstrable.

Still, the problem for many in this professional/managerial class is that to admit they are not indispensable is to admit they are not *better than*. For, make no mistake, there are still a whole lot of people in this world who are just fine with a *certain* number of human beings languishing on the margins, serving merely as fuel for the machine.

Come to think of it, maybe there are a few of you out there whom I want to take this personal.

But, for everyone else, just know that my satiric call for your loss is really a quite serious call for transition, transition into something better for us all. If I had it my way, we'd all lose our jobs. We'd all lose our jobs, we'd let the robots do the bulk of the non-fulfilling tasks, and we'd all start working towards making a contribution rather than making a living.

That's why when I cheer on the lawyerbots and doctorbots and accountantbots and whatnotbots, and call for more of those bots, I accompany those cheers and that call with a vision for a real alternative and an appeal for you to join us.

But that appeal is not only a welcome; it's a warning.

For, let me say this again. As long as there are institutions that recognize and respect obscene wealth disparity, those institutions will recognize and respect our own special brand of obscene power disparity. And you *know* what that disparity, what that consolidation of power, will inevitably translate to.

You still have a great deal of power. You *still* have time to use it.

Don't wait too long.

Anti-sermon 06
A Call to the Altar (Part Two): I Came Here to Proselytize

Fellow travelers

Now, before I move on with this last sermon, I want to acknowledge something for those who are not already aware of it. Although my prophetic vehicle may be slightly unconventional, I am certainly not the only one extolling the revolutionary potential of these new technologies. In fact, some of my fellow travelers believe a better world is closer than what I believe.

And while those fellow travelers may be offering proposals that are far less revolutionary, I applaud their achievement of fitting such radical technologies as nicely as they have into current institutions, while at the same time gearing their visions in the direction of *real* change.

Still, I do not share their optimism. Just because most of these proposals are pitched in a market-based package, we cannot assume capitalists are going to greet them with open arms.

On the contrary, I think the safer assumption is backlash and sabotage.

And it's not that the incentive they've laid out is unimpressive. It's that peace doesn't look like incentive to a war profiteer.

Furthermore, there is no reason to believe all relevant players will act rationally. It doesn't matter how much sense it makes on paper or if you can prove it worked in ten different models/experiments. When it comes to this kind of economic change, you can never make it rational enough. You're up against religion, and a very rigid sect at that.

I believe *our* vision can achieve an even better world than that of my fellow travelers. I believe theirs settles for too little, leaves the door open for rollbacks, and leaves us unprepared for the fight we will face.

Yet anyone who believes these critiques, our tactics, or even the better world I am proposing will somehow sully these less radical efforts has got it backwards. If anything, they make *those* efforts look that much more attractive.

I admit. Their scenario has a better shot at happening, and it *is* far more desirable than the current state of affairs. So to anyone who fears how radical my dreams are, you'd be wise to embrace theirs. These are your fucking Roosevelts, not in the sense that FDR championed the poor but that he saved capitalism.

We, on the other hand, are not here to save capitalism. While we may applaud the gains made by poor and working people under The New Deal, what *we* are championing is something else, something very different. Not because we do not believe that reforms are important. But because we believe there is no *deal* to be made when it comes to freedom, no deal to be made when it comes to human rights, no deal to be made when it comes to justice.

No.

We are not here to settle for reform; we are here to champion justice. A justice that you, the rich and powerful, have avoided too long, but one *we* can't avoid any longer.

Now, *I know* you're coming to fight. And *I know* you've got more power. I know that you're willing to do dirtier shit than we are, and that you'll get away with a lot of that dirty shit.

But I also know we've got something you can't guard against.

And that's creativity. You can't out-imagine us. You can't out-dream us. You can't out-envision us.

Because we are truly hungry, while you are mere gluttons.
The glutton doesn't need to eat; they only think they do.

We, on the other hand, need this.
We need this future. We need this victory.

(Hallelujah!?!)

(Hallelujah.)

Something no one ever saw coming
Now, when I say they can't guard against our creativity, I don't mean our individual creativity. I mean the creative force of our collective imagination.

Over time, the consolidation of money has made our numbers less intimidating, less powerful. And the only way to change that is to harness the creativity of our numbers, to find our solution in the accumulation of our talents, to find hope in the momentum of our solidarity.

In other words, we need all of you.

Not only is it foolish to wait for new heroes or for the resurrection of old ones, it's hubris to believe one person or even a few persons can know all the answers. It allows whoever can garner the most hope to stake claim on salvation and assume unwarranted authority, while the rest of us surrender our agency.

It also endorses the concept that we, as individuals, are so fundamentally limited that we have to look *up* for help, rather than to the person or persons by our side.

We are told the best we can do is to focus on ourselves. And then we wonder why there's a lack of political will.

Think about how counterproductive that mindset is to progress. And yet that is precisely why capitalists, and many libertarians, want us to think as individuals. By keeping people atomized, you completely limit their potential to be a part of something bigger, collectively and cooperatively.

And that's why it is so important that we develop technology right now that can emulate the intricate beauty of a swarm.

Imagine one million people asked, not to solve a complex problem, but to tackle a small portion of that problem according to their specific talents. The results of which would be arranged by algorithm and fit together like pieces of a photo mosaic, all according to how *we* have programmed what *we* want the final picture to look like.

We make random people not so random, and we combine our collective gifts into something otherwise unachievable.

It may be true that individually we only have so much potential. But just look at what ants do together, what bees do together, what coordinated beauty birds can create in the air together. With the right swarm infrastructure, these problems don't seem as daunting.

Our salvation is not hidden in the mind of some future mathematician, nor is it some pearl of spiritual insight only accessible to a sage or guru.

It's in our connection with one another. It's in recognizing our shared values and then using those principles to guide our questions. It's about inviting mass innovation, diverse innovation, until the best answers manifest.

I believe that the key to unlocking both political willpower and creative fury is to coral our asses into the swarm. And yes I believe that, once we are familiar and comfortable with such a process, we will harness this creative swarm to produce something no one ever saw coming.

And for those who worry this swarm concept sounds too much like conformity, it's not about conforming to a system. Neither is it conformity to any particular authority. It is merely a confirmation and adherence to shared values.

Believe me. I have no interest in a swarm for the status quo. What I want is a swarm that can scale the walls of this ideological prison and then bring those motherfucking walls tumbling down.

Gamification and the Swarm
"And how might we herd all the dodos into the swarm?" you ask.

Well, that's simple. We just invite everyone over for game night.

That's right. In the coming years, you're going to see gamification in areas never before imagined. Gamification of design, of programming, of problem solving.

You're going to see a gamification for the strategizing of resistance, gamification of cooperation and collaboration, gamification of efficiency and sustainability.

Imagine gamification that nurtures solidarity and counterbalances unhealthy competition.
Imagine gamified activism, where strategy is measured by results not just in the short term but over time, rewarded through the witness of progress.

Or maybe the reward will just be the challenge, the achievement of making it to that "next level" and taking down another "boss."

From the basics of survival all the way to that better world, we're going to get to the end. And we're going to have fun doing it.

The revolution may not be televised, but it sure as fuck will be gamified.

Beneath the drawbridge
Having said that, let us not fool ourselves into believing this is going to be easy.

We can use tools like gamification and swarm facilitation, not only to disrupt but to replace.
We can use encrypted, distributed infrastructure and the INDIEnet to make our maneuvers safer and less traceable.

From out-of-nowhere technological innovation to good old-fashioned guerilla protest, I believe we can find a way to win. But I do not want to romanticize the fight.

This is going to get messy.

There are no welcome mats at the castle door. There's a fucking drawbridge. And in the moat beneath the drawbridge are a bunch of hungry-ass dragons.

Revolution implies risk and requires sacrifice.

And if our strategy is partially comprised of actions that are not, shall we say, currently legal, then so be it. What public conversation has ever been changed by people simply obeying the law?

From lunch counter sit-ins to unsanctioned strikes to spontaneous occupations to post-injustice uprisings, this kind of disruption (almost always in some way illegal) is what it took to change the discourse and force people to pay attention and eventually make a stand one way or the other. This is no different.

While I foresee a Great Flood on the horizon, that Great Flood must be accompanied with communication that makes clear what the dangers are up ahead unless we liberate our collective intelligence.

Just like a riot is at times the only thing that can begin to bring about a needed discussion, we will need a Great Flood or maybe a few Great Floods.

But it is imperative we communicate in an honest and authentic manner; it is imperative that we provoke empathy and that we provoke questioning. For the only way we will be able to achieve a collaborative vision is if we get everyone asking questions.

But make no mistake. We are going to make some mistakes.

And that's why it's so important to make this movement as transparent as possible. That's why it's important we engage all those not directly involved in our movement. Because the public conversation which arises the day after an action is often far more important than the results of the action itself.

It is not enough for the public to simply be *aware* of our intentions. They must believe them. And the only hope we have of that happening is in the lessons we take from those missteps and how we demonstrate what it is that we've learned.

For this reason, we must look forward to our mistakes the same as we look forward to our victories. Not for the celebration or lack of on that day, but what we make out of it and where we take it the day after.

Today we sent thousands into the streets
(Let us pray.)

We can hold a march.
We can send thousands of people into the streets.
We can sing songs and chant chants.
We can wear costumes and hold up signs.
We can be peaceful and respectful.
We can be earnest and demonstrate the righteousness of our demands.

And then we can go home
and hope

that this time
their response will be different.

As if we have forgotten
the last march.
As if we have forgotten
the last hundred marches.
As if we have forgotten
they can wait
forever.

Your just cause doesn't guarantee you results.

Nor does marching peacefully guarantee your safety
or your freedom.

They've gotten used to the sting
of our numbers.
They've gotten used to the sounds
of our pain.
They've gotten accustomed
to our routine.
They've gotten good
at making it go away.

Just mollify
and move on.

Why are we still doing this
this way?

I'm not saying we shouldn't carry the past with us.
We should.
But we cannot commit to it.

If we believe
not just in the theory
but the practice of a better world
our movement
must foreshadow it.

The tools we use
to run our future system
are the tools we must use
in our struggle
to get beyond the current one.

This is not to say we should not march.
But if we are to march
it must be understood
what this is.

A gift.

We're allowing you the choice
to give back what is ours.

You will only get this option
once.

Today we sent thousands into the streets.
Tomorrow we send thousands into the swarm.

(Amen?)

(Amen.)

Pass around the bucket and raise a little hell

So I've talked a good deal about theory, and I've talked a good deal about strategy. But now it's time to talk about who's going to pick up the tab for our revolution. I think it goes without saying that, in a revolution, there is quite a lot to do. And if we're going to fund all that there is to do, it's initially going to require those of us with any economic privilege at all to step the fuck up.

So let's talk about how we do that. Let's talk about money. Until we get rid of it, we've got to talk about it.

If we want this to be more than just Karl Marx/Ursula Le Guin fan fiction, we're going to have to get fucking serious. We're going to have to invest not just in communal automation for both manufacturing and service needs, but in alternative allocation institutions that make these developments welcome for workers. We're going to have to find *and compensate* visionary coders, designers, and engineers to help develop the kind of democratized infrastructure in which to introduce these institutions. We're going to have to disseminate gamified simulators for economy and governance that allows for innovation from those with gifts not yet recognized. We're going to have to commit to an economic and/or resource endowment that ensures *our* model has a path.

In addition to that, we're going to have to start putting radical hardware into people's lives. We need to be building open source 3D printers and distributing them to neighborhood Share Labs, which in turn can, among so many other things, build these INDIEnet nodes and smartphone attachments for mass dissemination.

I like to think of it as a package deal for revolution.

And while some of this stuff could be sourced through philanthropic grants and foundation money, some of it is going to be so radical that the institutional do-gooders won't come near it.

Of course, that is one way to know whether your movement is truly revolutionary, when even figuring out how to pay for your actions becomes an exercise in revolution.

Now, obviously, we could start off with good old-fashioned retail fronts, things like pot shops and thrift stores, food trucks and pop-up spots. Co-op style operations that allocate a portion of their proceeds toward Damning the Man.

But that's just on the business side. Consumer funding may involve a voluntary tax system, where you prearrange to generously throw in an extra 1% on each of your credit card purchases to go toward fucking up the system. Or how about a donate-at-purchase system, where similar to getting asked to donate a dollar to the children's hospital when you're checking out at the grocery store (when the *only* reason we don't have fully funded universal healthcare is because the capitalists who run this system are some fucking bastards), imagine instead paying at your favorite taco joint and getting asked at the register, "Would you like to donate fifty cents to Crush The Bastards?"

Of course, if we are truly committed to crushing the bastards, then we're going to have to acknowledge: fuck everything having to be about business and transactions. Have some fun with it. Throw dance parties and block parties. Put on music shows and art shows. Pass around the bucket, and raise a little hell.

And it's not just individuals giving either. We need to think in terms of swarm funding.

Instead of Kickstarter, we need our own crowdfunding site/app dedicated to bankrolling a revolutionary wish list. We could call it Firestarter or Shitstarter.

And fuck making donations one at a time. Make it subscription-based, where folks get in the habit of choosing the actions they support but can't be physically involved in, allowing/forcing us to stay invested, both financially and mentally.

All of which could be nicely supplemented by operating an underground stable-coin crypto-lottery. Think of it like playing the numbers for a better world, or rather in pursuit of a world where no one needs lotteries.

And don't just think local either. We should be organizing for international activist unions to pool resources together and provide movement solidarity in the form of both action and funding.

And even that is not thinking big enough.

If, in the short term, we're still going to have advertising and we're still going to have currencies, why not create an app that overlays your current social media and allows you to negotiate consensual data trading and exposure to advertising, with a small fraction put toward escorting those still fucking around to a place of finally finding out.

That's the kind of shit it is going to take if we're going to be able to fund this revolution.

Like I said before, I don't have all the answers. These are just a few ideas that popped into my head while I was coming up with the sermon. But if a stupid motherfucker like me can come up with all these ideas, there's no reason why we *all* can't come together and figure this shit out.

I get by with a little help from my enemies

And if we still don't have enough after all that? Well, we'll just have to ask the capitalists for it.

Now, I know that sounds like a strange tactic, but bear with me.

While I believe that capitalism is on its way to completing humanity's doomsday device, I see the right combination of these new technologies as a potential doomsday device for capitalism.

The question is: How do you fund the building/development of a doomsday device for capitalism in a capitalist economy?

Well, one way is to do it on the cheap. Guerilla style, in the basement, tinkering and soldering with whatever scraps you have available, all in the starry-eyed hope of setting up the classic David vs. Goliath story where you take down the big bad corporations on a shoestring budget.

And for those who are out there right now giving that a shot, cheers to you.

Yet, personally, I think there's an even juicier story to be written.

I think you build the doomsday device completely out in the open. And you fund it by charging consulting fees to the very capitalists the device is aimed at.

Because, see, the people who build this device are going to be in high demand. And capitalists are going to spend literally billions of dollars, asking three basic questions. How does the device work? How can I save myself from the device? How can I co-opt the device?

And in their determination to find the answers to these three questions, they will neither know nor care who they're giving all this money to (namely, the people who built the device). And if they *do* know or they do care? Well, that won't really matter either, because they are not going to have a fucking choice.

Imagine that shit, y'all. Imagine *paying* someone to provide tech support for the computer virus *they* just infected you with. That shit is going to happen. That shit is happening right now.

Now, some might warn me not to say any of this too loud. Some might worry that if the capitalists get wind of these ideas, they might reverse course.

But I'm not worried about that. Because that's not our brand of capitalism.

Our brand of capitalism is one in which short term gains take full priority over future consequences. That's our brand of capitalism. That's how Michael Moore got capitalist film studios to produce and release an anti-capitalist movie.

And that is what the studios of Wall Street are going to do for us as well. They're going to produce our fucking movie. And they're going to produce that movie because that movie will prove to be a profits bonanza, at least on opening weekend.

See, the beautiful thing about having the titans investing so much in this technology is that they're going to find a way to make money with it. And the more money they make, the more they'll invest. All of which ensures two things.

Number one, not only are corporations going to cough up ungodly sums of cash to attract the brightest minds within the tech world, they're going to provide the resources necessary to raise the skills in said minds so high that it will only take a small group of outliers to figure out how to bring the whole thing tumbling down. In other words, the corporations are going to pay to be outsmarted. The banks are going to fund their own heist.

Number two, by the time they realize what's going on, it will be too late to stop it. They will have unwittingly protected our playground by legitimizing the technology. This is not to say they won't try; I'm sure they will. But it's pretty darn difficult to suddenly outlaw something today after you just made millions off it yesterday.

Pretty awesome, right? I can just see it on the big screen. *Best Heist Ever: A Story of Tech Hubris*. Where the rich are the ones with the master plan, spending every last dime to co-opt the promise of this new technology and steal from the people what may be their last chance at a better world. And I know what you're thinking. Having their own henchman turn into Robin Hoods is pretty darn predictable. But that's what makes the movie so great, that the directors didn't see this most obvious plot twist even as they were making the movie. And what was supposed to be the ultimate box-office blockbuster is ultimately what funded the studio's demise.

That is the movie I want to see. And that's the movie I believe we're going to see. Because I am a believer in poetic justice. And if there ever was poetic justice, it is that the seed capital for this revolution will have come from the bastards who could only see this technology for its weaponization, and never for its liberation.

(Hallelujah!?!)

(Hallelujah.)

Asking you to go beyond

So this is it.

I'm asking you to come with us. I'm asking you to go beyond.
I'm asking you to go beyond capitalism, because capitalism has already gone beyond us.
We don't factor into the equation. That's why we need a new equation.
I'm asking you to help write a new equation. I'm asking you to come with us.
I'm asking you to go beyond.

And if you think it is hyperbole when I say we do not factor into the equation, you need only imagine what measures will be taken to preserve this system, and to remember what measures have been taken before.

Just because the revolution I am describing is nonviolent in nature doesn't mean the reaction of capitalists will also be nonviolent.

Capitalism is not going to go gentle into that good night.

Like any revolution, this one *will* require sacrifice.
But unlike any revolution before it, we will be able to see results never before imagined.

I'm asking you to see what isn't yet there. I'm asking you to commit to making it real.
I'm asking you to come with us. I'm asking you to go beyond.

We can create a movement

And yet I know that creating political will is not as simple as shouting "WAKE UP" or throwing cold water into someone's face.

The mood in which someone awakes influences how receptive they will be to the one who woke them.

That is why it is so important that we *show* what going beyond capitalism can look like.
We have to provide a space for hope. We have to find and demonstrate a destination for hope.

If we are to win, that hope is a necessity. If we are to win, that hope is not optional.

Having said that, that hope must be measured. It must be grounded.

Because, see, after having felt hopeless for so long, it's going to be easy to want to *stay* in that place of hope.
But if we are to win, we cannot stay in that place too long.

I can tell you from my own experience that when you dive into this world for the first time, this world of radical technology, it is quite heady. The possibilities hit you almost in flashes. Moments of euphoria.

And you know what? We need those moments. Those moments of imagining, of dreaming, of seeing the promise being offered us.

But what we cannot do is become so enamored with the technology's potential that we lose sight of the darker side of our own.

They're developing bioanalytic tools right now that can monitor everything from the chemical levels in our brains to the sincerity of our smiles.

These devices *could* be used to help us measure effort and sacrifice for a more just system of compensation. Or these devices could be used to steal the last bit of one's autonomy in already horrendous working conditions.

There are different worlds.

Anyone who believes the technology will simply settle these questions for us *ensures* they will not be settled in our favor.

For it is not a matter of "If we don't do X, they are going to do Y." They are going to do what they are going to do anyway.

That is why hope is not optional. Hope is a necessity.

But it is going to take a whole lot of work, a whole lot of sacrifice, to turn that hope into something tangible, something real.

And that is why we need *all* of you.

I believe we can create a movement that cannot be defeated, no matter how many individuals are outspent, no matter how many individuals are sued or sanctioned, no matter how many individuals are imprisoned or killed.

I believe we can create that movement. But it will require you believing it too.

It will require your contribution, your commitment.

It will require you to respond to the call.

The call is nothing without the response
Any conductor will tell you. Any comedian will tell you. Any preacher will tell you. The call is nothing without the response.

I came here to evangelize. Not so you might follow me, but so you might recognize the gravity of this moment and follow your conscience.

As vain as I may be, I know this isn't about me. I'm not special. I'm not a leader. I'm just some dude.

As a young man, I wasted so much of my intellectual potential, I made so many mistakes, I did so many things wrong that I cannot take back. But I've realized *that* time was only wasted if I do not learn from it. It is only a waste if I do nothing right now.

I don't have the talent it takes to write this magnificent code. I don't have the smarts it takes to design these programs or to build these machines. All I have is this one shot at inspiring you to use your talents and your smarts for something bigger than us all.

I did not come here to create a cult.
I came here to make my contribution in creating a movement.

Cults are driven by a leader. Movements are driven by people.

This isn't about me.
This isn't about if I'm right.
It's about you.
It's about if you are willing to get behind what you *know* is right.

I came here to proselytize.
Not for you to have blind faith in a deity. But for you to have faith in humanity, and to have faith in yourself.

I'm not the only one making it, but goddamn it, I *am* making it. I'm making the call.

I pray that you will respond.

Afterword

I wrote the majority of *Revival* in 2017.

I let a few friends read the text when it was finished in 2018, and the response was not great. I let a few more friends hear an audio version of it in 2020, and the response was not great.

Critiques ranged from the preacher style being off-putting and the sermon format being wrong for the subject matter, to the feeling I had been too harsh on skeptics in the second anti-sermon, to worries I had discredited my good points by certain misplaced focus on points some felt were suspect, all the way to objections over my excessive use of curse words.

After that, I postponed again and again publishing *Revival* as a book. I even had the cover made up a couple years ago and still refrained from releasing it. Although I loved so much of what I wrote, I felt the work was a failure.

As any writer will tell you, one's choice of words at breakfast may bear no resemblance to one's choice at lunch. And with each year that's passed, with new events and information having accumulated alongside the natural development of my own ideas, I've wondered how these passages might have come out differently had I written them in a different season.

Nonetheless, while I am willing to concede to how much I got wrong, there's a lot I got right. Rereading it almost a decade later, so much of it is just as, if not more, relevant today. Hence my decision to go ahead with publication.

The question was whether to rewrite it in a more conventional style or to stick with the anti-sermons as they were originally crafted.

Aside from some minor tweaks before going to print (mostly to correct for my disproportionate emphasis on blockchain, and not enough emphasis on AI), I decided to pretty much keep it as-is. It doesn't mean I think my friends were wrong. In fact, I think the book could easily be seen as a failure for all the reasons they gave and more.

I kept it this way because I like it this way. I believe what I said in the introduction. We need both culture and common language. We need cadence and charismatic oratory. We need - our own version of church.

And, truthfully, we need more failures. We need more examples of people trying, and trying again. The more failures we have, the closer we get to winning.

But only if we learn to mine those failures for the value each has to offer. Both to carry forward what it is they got right and to explore the missteps for what they too add to the discussion. The key being to listen - in a curious humility, so we may better keep watch on how it is we are discerning between the two.

That's the way life is. And that's the way church should be.

The only thing I ask, and I acknowledge it's at the risk of wearing out my welcome, is that you take a few days to reflect on what you liked and didn't like in the work - and then read it again.

Read it again, and leave behind that which you do not find to be helpful. But take from it what will move your life *and this moment* forward, knowing that you too *will* help write this history.

Like any given Sunday monologue, these words are no more gospel than the action you put behind them. And as the best of parables demonstrate, there is power in dreaming.

It's my prayer that these pages might provide you - a little more space to do just that.

Lonnie Ray Atkinson
2025

www.ingramcontent.com/pod-product-compliance
Lightning Source LLC
LaVergne TN
LVHW022107200926
848481LV00003B/1095